Secrets of PI Agency Management

BY KELLY E. RIDDLE

Copyright © 2013
By
Kelly E. Riddle

All rights reserved. No part of this publication may be reproduced or transmitted in any form or by any means, electronic or mechanical, including photocopy, recording or any information storage and retrieval system, without permission in writing from the author, except for brief excerpts for reviews.

TABLE OF CONTENTS

Chapter 1	Time Management	page 3
Chapter 2	Using the Media	page 20
Chapter 3	Finding Your Niche	page 35
Chapter 4	The Power of the Written Word	page 41
Chapter 5	Associations	page 62
Chapter 6	The Power of the Spoken Word	page 69
Chapter 7	Character is Everything & Records	page 77
Chapter 8	Off the Wall Advertising	page 89
Chapter 9	How to Run a Successful Business	page 91
Chapter 10	Useful Forms	page 130
Chapter 11	Internet and Search Engine Marketing	page 143
Chapter 12	Effective Business Plans	page 159
Chapter 13	Residual Income	page 177
Chapter 14	The Real Secret to Success	page 180
Chapter 15	About the Author	page 184

TIME MANAGEMENT
Chapter One

The "job" of being a private investigator is the end result of fundamental business skills coupled with proper psychological and operational skills. Before you can be successful as a private investigator, you first need to tackle areas that you most assuredly require some fine-tuning. It is absolutely essential to understand and utilize time management techniques. Just as important is your ability to function with the right mind-set.

At the very basic level, you first have to obtain business (clients and cases). This requires you to have the ability to market your skills, develop a professional reputation and set the stage *for* business. Once you receive an assignment, your capacity to function as a private investigator and to develop into a leader is critical to insuring you get additional work. Your mind and attitude is a battlefield that you must conquer and control. We will therefore discuss these elements, for without them, no amount of marketing will prevail.

By now, everyone has heard of time management and knows the concept. However, to become the #1 PI, you have to really grasp that concept. While your friends are enjoying the 4th of July or are watching TV, you will be the one working away at your computer. To be extremely successful, you will probably have to have a type "A" personality and no doubt be a workaholic. You will have to learn how to juggle three or four different things at the same time. Sounds easy, right? Sounding and doing are two entirely different issues. From the moment I really set out to move to the top of the industry, it took 4-5 years of intense work. This is not one of those things that happened over-night. It is like a child that is born and grows over a long period of time. If you are not ready to devote the time, and I mean a lot of time, you may as well not even start down the path.

Time management[1] and time-motion techniques are similar and have direct bearing on the success of any business. Time management is a technique credited as being founded by Frederick Winslow Taylor[2] (March 20, 1856 – March 21, 1915). Taylor was an American mechanical engineer and is regarded as the father of scientific management. He sought to improve industrial efficiency and was one of the first management consultants. A time and motion study[3] (or time-motion study) is a business efficiency technique combining the Time Study work of Frederick Winslow Taylor with the Motion Study work of Frank and Lillian Gilbreth. Time study is a direct and continuous observation of a task, using a timekeeping device (e.g., decimal minute stopwatch) to record the time taken to accomplish a task. It is often used when:

- there are repetitive work cycles of short to long duration,
- there is a wide variety of dissimilar work is performed, or
- process control elements constitute a part of the cycle.

To better understand this concept, a study was conducted by NBM Construction Information[4] regarding the placement of rebar at a construction site. The study found the optimum number of personnel for rebar placement is 10 - 12 on the work location. The optimum number of human resources assigned for construction activities leads to economy, reduction in time and quality work. The study identified essential and non-essential work:

Category	Study Number						
	1	2	3	4	5	6	7
Direct work	60.02%	71.27%	61.75%	71.22%	68%	70.53%	70.08%
Essential contributory work.	20.98%	17.10%	18.82%	15.51%	17.7%	14.00%	15.48%
Ineffective work	19.0%	11.63%	19.43%	13.27%	14.3%	15.47%	14.44%

---

[1] http://en.wikipedia.org/wiki/Time_and_motion_study
[2] http://en.wikipedia.org/wiki/Frederick_Winslow_Taylor
[3] http://en.wikipedia.org/wiki/Time_and_motion_study
[4] http://www.nbmcw.com/articles/case-studies/28978-time-and-motion-study-analysis-through-statistics.html

Categories are further subdivided into narrowly defined categories of activity as follows:

- Direct or Effective Work:-

    1. Direct work—Place, align, force, and tie into position plus those Elements which contribute directly to completing the unit of work.

- Essential Contributory Work-

    2. Obtain or transport tools and materials within immediate vicinity of work area including torch, sledge, wire cutters, rigging, reinforcement tie wire, etc. Also includes searching for materials. The immediate vicinity is defined as the existing concrete mat. The staging area is excluded.

    3. Obtain or transport tools and materials outside of immediate vicinity of work area including all tool and material movement not in close proximity to the work location. Activities in the staging area are included.

    4. Includes activities associated with crane deliveries until such time as the lift actually begins.

    5. Receive/give instructions and read drawings involving instructions communicated to or by supervisors and among crew members. Casual talking is not considered instructions. Also included is the studying of drawings and planning work. Foreman in staging area looking for materials is considered as planning work.

    6. Minor contributory work measuring or marking bar location, holding a bar to prevent movement, cutting w/torch, moving scaffolding, etc.

- Ineffective Work-

7. Travel empty-handed to and from the work area and within the work area, either on foot or in a vehicle.

8. Idle, unexplained waiting that cannot be accounted for. Distinction between idle and waiting for prerequisite activity or craft is if worker is in a position to assist, he is waiting for prerequisite work, otherwise, unexplained. Includes personal time while in the immediate vicinity of the work location.

9. Waiting for tools, materials, instructions, crane deliveries, prerequisite work, other crafts, etc. Workers should be in position to continue work when the delay ends.

10. No contact—failure to observe worker who is assigned to a specific work location. Includes early quit, late start, and time away from the immediate work location.

As an example from a PI example, in my earlier years in business my day usually consisted of working 14-16 hours a day both in the field and in the office. I typically started out around 6:00-6:30 A.M. and worked with some of my investigators doing surveillance until around 11:30 A.M. I would then leave them and go take some clients out to lunch. After this, I would head to the office where I spent time doing administrative tasks and returning phone calls. I would try to spend at least an hour a day marketing, which I will go into later. By this time, the time would be creeping up around 4:00 P.M. so I either review files or go back into the field to continue investigations. I would get home around 6:00-6:30 P.M. and take about 30 minutes to eat dinner. After this I would resume work in my study at the house until around 9:30-10:00 P.M. I would get up the next day and start it all over again. Of course, my day varied based on speaking engagements, cases and other factors that cause me to adjust the hours I allot for certain functions and duties. I am fortunate to be one of those people who can

talk on the telephone, check my regular mail and work on the computer all at the same time. This ability allows me to get even more duties compressed into my day. Since the company has grown, my duties have also had to change and my time in the field has had to diminish.

I find myself developing time management habits without even realizing it. If I am going to run a check through the Secretary of State's records, I check all 3 or 4 people that I am doing backgrounds on at the same time even if they are totally different cases. I have each document open and I can quickly cut and paste information into each. If I am going to walk to the front of our offices to give something to my office manager, I take a DVD and drop it in a case manager's office, pick up a new package of copy paper, shred a document and anything else I can do between my office and the front. I put things like this on the corner of my desk so when I do get up, all can be done in one trip. Sounds trivial, but this enables me to stay focused and allows my time to be optimized.

A big obstacle to a successful career and a successful life is *you*. If you don't have the right thinking and the right attitude, you can be your biggest stumbling block. Business is not easy and if it were, everyone would be in business for themselves. There are some key areas that must be developed if you ever have hope of being successful. These include:

1) Attitude

2) Initiative

3) Commitment

4) Sacrifice

5) Passion

6) Integrity

7) Consistency

8) Prioritization

9) Spiritual Strength

10) Perseverance

Some people would lump many of these together and confuse their distinct nature, which would be a mistake. The ability to get all of these lined up and working in unison provides the well-oiled machine that can carry out great tasks. We will therefore take the time to discuss each.

Attitude

Attitude has to do with what comes out of your mouth. If you go around talking about doom and gloom that is what you will become. It is easy to look at the glass half-empty or you can look at it half full. The decision is your decision, your attitude is your attitude and your success (or lack of it) is strictly up to you.

Time management is very closely related to attitude. You have to either have the right attitude or develop the attitude. When you decide to set aside the tremendous amount of time to reach the goal, your attitude is what will keep you going or stop you in your tracks. If you are one of those people who are easily distracted and who moves from project to project without finishing what you start, you probably won't achieve this goal either. It requires time allotment, the right attitude, persistence and consistency. Working investigations is only a percentage of the whole picture. You will have to be able to provide a great work product just to stay in business, but to become the #1 PI, this only accounts for about one-third of the entire process. Attitude is what drives you to go the extra step, to spend a little more time and to over-look the difficulties. If you can't harness your attitude and make it work for you then you will fail before you begin. The attitude that prevails consists of an almost perfectionist out-look that causes you to move forward and be harder on yourself than you would be on anyone else. Harness the attitude and you're on your way. Let your attitude beat you and failure is pending.

I have been around people who seem to complain all the time. We have all seen this and we run the opposite way when we see them coming. This person has allowed himself or herself to develop a self-defeating attitude. I have been around a lot of investigators like that. All they do is complain about how bad business is and how they don't know what they are going to do if things don't get better. In fact, I have even been on the golf course with some of my competitors and mutual clients and have heard them complaining about business in front of the clients! Everyone wants to be around people that are upbeat and successful. No one likes a loser or complainer.

It takes more effort to complain than it does to reply in a positive manner. A study conducted by the Department of Biological and Clinical Psychology at Friedrich Schiller University in Germany[5] revealed that being in the presence of negative people or people who are complaining constantly caused the subjects' brains to have the same emotional reactions that they experienced when they were under stress. The term 'negativity bias' refers to the psychological phenomenon based on our tendency to pay more attention to negative entities, which might be in the form of events, traits, objects, etc. Studies have proved that the brain's reaction to negative stimuli is far more intense than the positive stimuli. We are more likely to remember or focus on negative things than positive ones. If complaining evokes similar response in the brain as stress, it's certainly not good for your health.

"Do not let any unwholesome talk come out of your mouths, but only what is helpful for building others up according to their needs, that it may benefit those who listen."[6] Again, the half-full or half-empty scenario applies. Your talk should be positive. That doesn't mean you have to ignore problems but you certainly should not focus on the problems. As an example, I was recently at the firing range and after completing the task, I was talking to the Range Instructor. He had an extremely positive attitude and was talking about going back to the Middle-East as a civilian contractor. He raised his pants legs to show two prosthetic devices and explained how he was in the Marines and his vehicle hit an IUD. Everyone in the vehicle was killed except him. You would never have known this from his speech as he was extremely positive.

As an employer, you have to keep both your attitude in check for you personally as well as for your employees. If you are positive, you will attract

---

[5] www.Buzzle.com
[6] Ephesians 4:29 (NIV)

people with a positive outlook. The last thing you need is to have a group of employees feeding off of one another's poor attitudes. You are the leader so you have to set the tone.

Initiative

Initiative is defined as, "An introductory step (2) energy or aptitude displayed in action (3) at one's discretion."[7] This is often where a person's good intentions die a slow death. "Day dreaming about something in order to do it properly is right, but daydreaming about it when we should be doing it is wrong."[8] To put it another way; your employees cannot follow a parked car. People have often asked me, "Why do you give all of your secrets away?" My answer is simple; "Because few have the initiative to get and go do it." It takes a great deal of initiative coupled together with discipline to continue to move forward. "A little sleep, a little slumber, a little folding of the hands to rest and poverty will come on you like a bandit and scarcity like an armed man."[9] It is much easier to sit in the chair and watch TV or to go play golf.

Wasting time is in direct competition with initiate. A new study from Kansas State University suggests that we spend even more time than previously thought aimlessly browsing the Internet during our office hours. "Cyber-loafing" — wasting time at work online — takes up as much as 80 percent of the time people spend online at work, according to the data collected by Joseph Urgin, an assistant professor at Kansas State, and John Pearson, an associate professor at Southern Illinois University.[10]

According to a recent Salary.com survey[11], one of the biggest culprits is surfing the Internet. Excessive meetings, co-worker interactions, office politics, and fixing mistakes are a few. More specifically, the survey revealed:

---

[7] Merriam-Webster Dictionary
[8] Oswald Chambers
[9] Proverbs 6:10 (Oxford NIV)
[10] http://news.yahoo.com/blogs/sideshow/much-80-percent-time-spent-online-wasted-according-235416254.html
[11] www.Forbes.com

1) 64 percent of employees visit non-work related websites *every day* at work.

2) Of that group, 39 percent spend one hour or less per week

3) 29 percent spend 2 hours per week

4) 21 percent waste five hours per week

5) And only 3 percent said they waste 10 hours or more doing unrelated activities.

The survey also revealed which websites keep employees most off-task. The results indicated:

1) socializing on Facebook occupied 41 percent

2) LinkedIn accounted for 37 percent

3) And 25 percent are shopping at Amazon. Other destinations include Yahoo and Google+ and to a lesser extent Twitter and Pinterest.

The younger, more tech-savvy worker demographic appeared to be the biggest group of recreational Web surfers. Of employees between the ages of 18 and 35, approximately 73 percent reported spending time inappropriately at work on a daily basis.

Respondents said the Number 1 reason for slacking at work was that they don't feel challenged enough in their job. Other reasons include, (2) they work too many hours, (3) the company doesn't give sufficient incentive to work harder, (4) they are unsatisfied with their career, and (5) they're just bored.

These reasons in part also explain why 46 percent of workers look for a new job while at their current place of employment. LinkedIn is the website of choice for those trying to network.

This information serves to confirm that it is easier to waste time than it is to take the initiative and apply yourself at being successful. As an employee, "Whatever you do, work at it with all your heart, as working for the Lord, not for men, since you know that you will receive an inheritance from the Lord as a reward. It is the Lord Christ you are serving."[12] As an entrepreneur and owner,

---

[12] Colossians 3:23 (Oxford NIV)

you are to set the example. I have changed light bulbs, used the vacuum, and cleaned the sink and anything else that needed to be done at the office. If you will not set the example then there is no example to follow.

Many people have a "wishbone" instead of a "backbone" – you need to stop wishing and start acting. Take control and decide where YOU want to go and how you want to get there. Take the initiative to get up and get going!

Commitment

Plain and simple, commitment is the difference between loosing and winning. Most often you hear about people being afraid to commit to a relationship. Likewise there are those who subconsciously fear failing and therefore do not set out in business. There are different types of commitment:

Commitment may refer to:

- A Promise, or personal commitment

- A Contract, a legally binding exchange of promises

- Brand commitment

- Organizational commitment

By definition commitment is, "A pledge to do. (b) Something pledged, especially an engagement by contract involving financial obligation or (3) the state of being bound emotionally or intellectually to a course of action or to another person or persons."[13] To start a business you have a certain amount of financial commitment required to get the proper licenses, insurance, equipment and start-up capital. Emotionally you will need to do a "gut-check" to see if you have the necessary commitment to stick through tough times because there *will* be tough times. Unfortunately, we live in a throw-away culture. If it no longer fits into our life or is to inconvenient, simply discard it. Failing in business can have a devastating effect on your finances as well as your emotions. "Commit to the

---

[13] www.FreeDictionary.com

Lord whatever you do, and your plans will succeed. The Lord works out everything for his own ends-even the wicked for a day of disaster."[14]

Entering into business requires commitment on your part. It is not to be done lightly. Not only will your family depend on your leadership but the employees and families of those that you employ will put their trust in you to be a leader who can master finances and business.

Sacrifice

Anything worthy of achieving requires sacrifice. By definition, sacrifice is "To suffer a loss, an act of offering something precious."[15] It may be something as simple as giving up sleep to get up early for surveillance. It may be paying employees before you have sufficient income to pay yourself. The sacrifice may involve difficulties in your relationship with your spouse due to your erratic schedules. Whatever the sacrifice, you will have to endure. Giving up is simply not a choice.

If you are in business long enough, you may have to go through an audit by the PI licensing authority, the IRS or State Comptroller. You may have to endure a lawsuit, complaint with the Better Business Bureau or some other attack. You will most likely have to pay subcontractors or employees for sub-standard work. Through these sacrifices you will endure and become stronger. A friend once told me "Don't worry, they can torment you but they can't eat you." Everything has to be put into perspective. At the time that the battle is raging, it may seem like the world is crashing down around you. You may have to sacrifice the battle to win the war. The sacrifice may be a short stumbling block on a long career.

"Nothing shapes your life more than the commitments you choose to make. Your commitments can develop you or they can destroy you. Either way they will define you."[16]

---

[14] Proverbs 16:3-4 (Oxford NIV)
[15] Merriam-Webster dictionary
[16] Rick Warren – "The Purpose Driven Life"

Passion

Over the years I have heard people say something like, "I don't know what I want to do with my life." This is fine as not everyone knows what they want to do from the time they were a kid. I am one of those that knew as far back as I can remember. That being said, if you are entering the PI profession out of curiosity or you just need a job, my advice would be simply "don't." Find your passion because whatever you are passionate about you will be good at and you will want to spend as much time doing this as possible. "Enthusiasm is one of the most powerful engines of success. When you do a thing, do it with all your might. Put your whole sole into it. Stamp it with your personality. Nothing great was ever achieved without enthusiasm."[17] The mere definition of passion drives this point home further, "Passion is when you put more energy into something than is required to do it. It is more than just enthusiasm or excitement, passion is ambition that is materialized into action to put as much heart, mind body and soul into something as is possible."[18] If the thought of being a private investigator does not totally excite you and if you are not willing to put all of your being into it, take time to consider if this is your path.

Integrity

As a private investigator, you will come face-to-face with issues that may impact your integrity. The manner in which you handle them will determine how long you will be in business and may even rise to the level of whether or not you go to jail. You character and your integrity will be the foundational blocks that your business is built upon. In the late 1990's I saw the need for the integrity level within the PI profession to be raised. I therefore founded the Association of Christian Investigators as an association where those of like faith could communicate openly. This is also one of the reasons why I belong to more than twenty PI related associations.

I have watched over the decades I have been in the profession as investigator after investigator lost their moral compass and got caught-up in criminal violations. They entered into the "gray" area and before you know it, were

---

[17] Ralph Waldo Emerson
[18] http://www.urbandictionary.com

operating in illegal activities by placing electronic bugs on telephones, becoming involved in staging fake evidence and similar tactics. Their moral compass may have been bad from the beginning but most likely they got emotionally tied to the client. In doing so they felt the need to help the client since they were the "expert" and the client was demanding results.

You will have ample opportunities for your integrity to be tested. You may have to follow a person into a men's club, go into a bar, and get a massage to determine the extent of their services or a host of other situations that PIs may find in their line of duty. Clear up any concern about your reaction to this now before you are faced with the particular situation.

When it comes to advertising, you should also maintain a high level of integrity. "Never write an advertisement which you wouldn't want your family to read. You wouldn't tell lies to your own wife. Don't tell them to mine."[19] The PI profession has enough issues with integrity. It is much better to present a professional image, to maintain your integrity and not use the filth and sleaze that accompanies many advertisements.

Consistency

Consistency is a value that was taught to me early in my high school days by my coach. I had been placed on the varsity basketball team as a sophomore. Unfortunately, one game I would start and the next I may not get but a couple of minutes of playing time. One day in aggravation I went to my coach to find out why I was being used like a yo-yo. His reply was simple. He indicated that I was not consistent and advised that one-day I would play at the top of my ability and then the next I couldn't find my way out of the locker room. The coach indicated that I either needed to be consistently good, or consistently bad, but he had to know what to expect from me whenever I was on the floor. By the end of my senior year, the coach described me in the newspaper as "Mr. Consistent." I had developed one of the best field goal and free throw percentages in the history of the school had become 4th in all time rebounding and set a new school record for most points in a single game. The concept of "consistency" became a way of life for me. I mean, think about it, your clients want a consistent work product and

---

[19] David Ogilvy

your friends and family need to know what to expect from you and how you will react to certain circumstances. This is an important factor in our daily lives as well as the success of our business.

By definition, consistency is "adhering to the same principles, course, form (b) capable of being reproduced (c) the same throughout in structure or composition (d) reliable." [20] One way that companies like McDonald's, Starbucks, Coca-Cola and Chick-Fil-A have dominated their international markets and done so well through consistency. They have the same product and quality over and over again. These companies have learned that having a consistent product and service would allow this to be duplicated, and then duplicated again. In doing so, they have been able to grow into world-wide organizations. Putting this into perspective as a PI, you should strive to provide the same look in your reports, the same results, and the same great work product and insure this happens each time you conduct an investigation.

Prioritization

People who don't know their purpose try to do too much; resulting in fatigue, stress and conflict. The way you *see* your life *shapes* your life. How you define life determines your destiny. Your perspective will influence how you prioritize and invest your time as well as how you use your talents. "Without a clear purpose you have no foundation on which you base decisions, allocate your time and use your resources. You make choices based on circumstances, pressures and your mood."[21]

Great opportunities may come around once in a life time but every day you have small opportunities that are presented. If a person is ever going to achieve anything great there will be times when they must risk everything and take a leap. Experience is a doorway to great things, not a final destination. Learning how to prioritize is a key to reaching the goals that you set. Motion for the sake of motion is simply false success. We must identify our purpose and then the process that helps achieve the purpose. Leaders must craft opportunities for others to become involved. Leadership should be clear about the process and be

---

[20] http://www.definitions.net
[21] Rick Warren – "The Purpose Driven Life"

committed to executing it. The process should flow logically and all of the staff should be arranged around the process/concept.

"Absolute identity with one's cause is the first and greatest condition of successful leadership."[22] A good leader must be able to lead and to follow. Their strengths compliment others instead of contradicting or being in competition. "The test of an organization is not genius. It is its capability to make common people achieve uncommon performance."[23] If a leader cannot infect others with a sense of purpose and urgency, the momentum will die short of completion. Battles can be won or lost by hanging on just a little bit longer. As a leader, you have an obligation to not declare your fears and doubts. The same energy it takes to retreat may be just the amount of energy needed to succeed. The leader must set the stage, create the pace and communicate enthusiasm for running the race.

"Success is never final and failure is rarely fatal. It is the courage to continue that counts."[24] Prioritization is a tool in the leader's tool bag that helps adhere to moving forward.

The leader has a responsibility to organize and prioritize. Others take their cue from the leader. Like the leader in a pack of long distance runners, your pace will establish the pace of those following.

Spiritual Strength

I recently heard a friend who used to be a PI and who is a minister talk about what comes out of your mouth. It struck me while listening to the message delivered by Mark Jones that some of our members might be guilty of poisoning their own business by projecting negative messages. This message is a powerful and useful tool that we can all use. If you need a blessing, claim it through the authority of The Word. EX: (Psalm 21:2) "You have granted him the desire of his heart and have not withheld the request from his lips." Two-thirds of God's name spells the word "go." It does not spell "fall" and no where will you see where God stands for failure. The Lord told us to go and heal, go and overcome

---

[22] Woodrow Wilson
[23] Peter Drucker
[24] Winston Churchill

sin, go and be prosperous. God never wanted us to do "nothing," but instead, told us to go and do good things in His name. We are told in John 14:13 "And I will do whatever you ask in my name, so that the Son may bring glory to the Father. [14] You may ask me for anything in my name, and I will do it." Praying about your problems is only complaining in repetition. God knows your problems. Speak your need and then speak God's word to overcome the need by confessing out loud and agreeing with the Word. Speaking the Word is agreeing with God's Word.

Many times you will hear someone say, "God works in mysterious ways." This is not true if you know the Word. You will know His voice. By saying something like, "I was so afraid I thought I was going to have a heart-attack," you are promoting negative actions that your mind and heart will start to believe. Fear is the enemy of faith. That doesn't mean you should deny someone is sick or there is a problem. Instead, deny the right for the sickness or problem to be there and speak the Word of God to overcome it.

You often hear people say, "If it wasn't for Church, I wouldn't get fed at all." Church is where you should go to get fine-tuned. You need to "study to show yourself approved" and when the time comes, "you can stand and fight the good fight." In business, as in our personal lives, we often have a tendency to compare our businesses or our lives to someone else's. When you hear other investigators complaining about how bad business is you have a tendency to get in the sinking boat with them. You can't base your faith on what happens to someone else. God gave us His Word as an example as well as an instrument or a tool in which to use.

Perseverance

Perseverance is another characteristic that the investigator will have to harness if they intend to become one of the top PI's in the profession. It is similar to what we have all heard about pit bull dogs. Once they grab hold, they never let go. There is another scripture that is worth repeating here. James 1:2-6 says, "Consider it pure joy, my brothers, whenever you face trials of many kinds, because you know that the testing of your faith develops perseverance. Perseverance must finish its work so that you may be mature and complete, not lacking anything. If any of you lacks wisdom, he should ask God, who gives generously to all without finding fault, and it will be given to him." A similar verse is James 1:12, "Blessed is the man who perseveres under trial, because when he has stood the test, he will receive the crown of life that God has promised to those who love him." To say it another way, you are going to face troubles, but if you do not persevere, you may miss those things that are just on the other side of the problem. Some of you have already experienced perseverance whether or not you realized it. Take for example the guy that you just lost on surveillance. You kept checking all the nearby businesses and streets until you stumbled across him again.

The truth is---private investigations are a business. Few _really_ understand this statement and _even fewer_ do anything about it.

Decide what you want to achieve----then decide how to get there. Things don't _just happen_. YOU are the one who will or will not achieve your goals.

Visualize Your Goal → Write it Down → Speak it → Achieve it

You can see how all of these things are closely related and how they must work together to be successful. One is as important as the other, and each form a limb of the entire body that allows the overall goal to be accomplished. The question that needs to be answered right here and right now is, "I am willing to put everything into this to be successful?" If not, why even bother to start down that path?

USING THE MEDIA
Chapter Two

I often have people ask me, "How do you manage to get on TV and radio programs all the time?" It is somewhat of an art, but it is just as much out of necessity; *their necessity* as much as mine. I had a friend who worked for one of the local TV stations and another with one of the radio stations. Both helped me understand the behind-the-scenes mind set of the media. TV and radio stations are in business to make money. To do this, they have to stay on top of breaking news and events that are of interest to the majority of their listening audience. They have to fill their programs daily with something "new" and of interest. You try thinking up new things to talk about every day of the year, year after year! It's difficult to put a new slant on an old story. These stations are begging for something worthwhile to beat their competition with and are more than eager to talk to private investigators.

"Advertising may be described as the science of arresting the human intelligence long enough to get money from it."[25] The ability to "arrest the human intelligence" gets harder and harder in a society driven by visual stimuli. Often the advertisement can be so simple that it is a refreshing breeze in the midst of the ocean of over-bearing advertisements. On the opposite spectrum, an advertisement may shock the senses, evoke emotions or be so cutting edge that it begs attention. The Super Bowl is the epitome of advertising as millions tune in as much for the commercials as for the football. Each commercial is heavily anticipated with great wonder to see if it is "the one" that everyone will be talking about the next day.

One of the most ridiculous statements that I hear some investigators make is something like, "I will never get involved with the media because they always miss-quote you." I can tell you from experience that this has only happened to me on one occasion and was nothing earth shattering. Each time I am on a program, my telephone won't stop ringing for a couple of weeks. This brings me to the next subject. If you are going to go through the trouble of promoting yourself and your business, it is crazy not to have someone ready to answer your

---

[25] Stephen Butler Leacock

phone calls. It doesn't do any good to go out and drum up business if there is no one *ready to take* the business. Each time I have an article published in a newspaper, I get calls from that one article six months to a year later. People will put the article aside knowing that one-day they will need your services or may want you to speak at a function. When I hear an investigator make statements about not using the media, my mind typically goes to several reasons behind this mindset. I think what they are really saying is that they don't know how to use the media or they are too lazy to do so. You're talking about <u>free</u> advertising.

I hear investigators say something like, "you can't be effective as a PI if your picture is plastered all over the place." My photograph is on a lot of my books and with all of my TV and written exposure, I have yet to have someone recognize me. This is kind of like the teenager who thinks they can drive recklessly because car accidents "won't happen to me." Most people have no idea they are being investigated, if you are doing your job right. The majority also think that being investigated "won't happen to them".

Of course, if you are going to be involved with the media, you have to set certain standards. There is a right way and a wrong way to be used by the media. The wrong way is going on TV and telling about how easy it is to get medical records, credit reports and other information that is illegal to have without a written consent. When you provide an interview, you have to balance the information to prevent our profession from being tarnished while at the same time providing some tantalizing information for the viewers. For instance, if you are talking about Internet investigations there is nothing wrong with explaining some of the information that is available on the Internet. However, you should also explain how this is monitored, how investigators use the information and that the information can also be obtained through normal public record channels. Everyone likes to see the latest and greatest technology but you should not disclose anything that is not fairly common knowledge as it simply makes it harder for every PI to do their job.

The underlying concept of an interview is to balance the interview with a dash of Hollywood combined with a bit of realism and public education. When an investigator is interviewed and tells how they can get all kinds of illegal information, it is a temporary self-serving situation that ultimately stains their reputation. This causes scrutiny of the industry and has caused legislation to pop-up in an attempt to limit access to information and records. If you are going to be involved with the media, you absolutely have to maintain your integrity. This will give everyone a better response to you and will provide you much more benefit in the long run.

There are several ways to approach a local TV station to seduce them into putting you on their programs. There are also different shows that you need to solicit that air at different times of the day. Part of your approach should include being somewhat familiar with the programs they have to offer. As an example, my first exposure to TV came at 6:00 A.M. Most channels have a morning show with their local television personalities. These shows spend a lot of time talking about the weather, traffic conditions and news stories. Remember, they are trying to appeal to the largest audience possible, so they often have people from local pet stores on with some animals to show. They also may have someone who has some insight into financial matters or similar guests. I approached them with the idea of discussing my first book, which dealt with teaching the general public how to find lost loved ones, using public records and things that would be beneficial to the average person. I sent the station a letter addressed to the program manager and several days later they were calling to arrange a date for me to be on the program. Needless to say, you have to get up early to be at the station by 5:45 A.M. and look all bright and chipper.

When you are asked to be on a TV program such as this, you can rest assured that it will not be what you expected. If the program airs at 6:00 A.M., they will want you to be there no later than 5:45 A.M. Getting in the building at that time of the morning can be a miracle in itself. After you get inside, they usually have someone who is in a hurry and who escorts you to a small waiting room. Not long after that, someone will stick their head in long enough to tell you that you will not be going on until near the end of the program around 6:45 A.M. You get the joy of sitting there almost an hour before getting your 2-3 minutes of stardom. The program moves at a quick pace and just before you go on, they will escort you to your seat in front of the camera, put a microphone on you, introduce you to the host and away you go. I have sense found that it is a good idea to send them some "sample" questions that you think might be advantageous for the host to glance through before the interview. This depends a lot on the host and how good of an interviewer the host is as well as how much they know about the subject.

Since the initial exposure to TV, I have sense approached the program director and have been on the program showing off some of the "spy gadgets" that are commonly used in our industry. They love this as everyone has the preconceived "James Bond" idea of PI's. If you have concealed video cameras, counter-measures devices, night vision or other tools of the trade, this is perfect for a "show and tell" segment. However, remember not to demonstrate anything that is still an unknown. If you do, the next time you try to use it in a covert manner those around you may be more suspicious. The key is to give them a little bit of flash, while keeping it real. If there is some type of incident in the news, figure out how an investigator could be used and give your thoughts to the media. They may pick up on it and use you and your information.

The media is a business, just like being a PI is a business. Once you grasp that, you have a better frame of mind and can realize that they need you just as much as you need them. The key is to be there at the right time. Part of this may be due to your advertising with their media. If you are paying them to advertise, they are much more likely to consider working with you on other things as well. However, I have found that marketing on the radio or on TV is expensive and does not provide good results. Part of this is due to the fact that we do not have a product that the majority of the audience needs and will not rush out to buy. If you had advertised blue jeans, sunglasses or something else, the audience may respond immediately. Unfortunately, our business is kind of like an air conditioner repair service. They don't need you until they have a problem. Because of this fact, radio and TV advertising will only work if you are willing to spend $10-20,000 a year to keep a steady advertising campaign going. To illustrate a point, what do you think of when you hear the words "Coca-Cola" or "McDonalds?" Exactly, you immediately know who they are and what their product is all about. That is because they spend millions of dollars to advertise continually. They also have a product that someone will buy immediately based on an emotional response.

So what should you expect to pay for advertising? This all depends on the market size, the size of the media station, when you want to air the advertisement, how many segments you purchase and the length of the advertisement. Incidentally, always ask the media sales representative to give you the "agency discount." This is a $10-15% discount that they give to an advertising agency and one that they will also pass on directly to the advertiser if you inquire about it. The size of the market sets the foundation for the cost of advertising. If you are advertising in one of the Top 10 markets, you can expect to pay more than for the same advertisement in a much smaller area. Although this is often associated with the demographic number of people in one area, size can be misleading. If the broadcast signal reaches neighboring counties and out-laying areas, the number of people that actually hear the message may be more than the immediate number of people in the city limits. The market size is a ranking that is established based on the number of people over a wide area who have the opportunity to view the information and not solely on the number of people in the immediate area.

The size of the media outlet is also of concern. If you have three local TV stations or radio stations, the one that has the most number of viewers will also be the most expensive station to place your advertisement. It is the law of supply and demand. Although you may get a better deal with one of the other stations, you should consider your ultimate goal, which is to reach as many people as possible. You may not see the trees for the forest in this situation.

One way that you can control cost is based on the time of day you want the advertisement to run. Obviously, anything after midnight is cheaper because there are less people up to view it. If you want the advertisement to run in the middle of the day while one of the top shows airs, you will pay much more for this. If running a TV advertisement after midnight, you can get the spots for as little as $15.00 each. However, running the same advertisement at 11:30 A.M. or 8:00 P.M. will cost $250 or more for each time it airs. The number of "spots" that you buy directly influences the price of the advertising. If you sign up for enough up front, they may even through in some additional spots in the less desirable time periods for free. The length of the advertisement is important as well. Usually, you can have a 15, 30 or 60-second advertisement. The longer the spot, the more it will cost.

Most TV stations will charge an extra fee to tape a commercial for you. Once again, if you contract for a longer period of advertisement, you may get this cost thrown in as well. The radio stations are easier to work with because it is easier to make the audio. Seldom will you get charged anything additional for this taping. It doesn't hurt to bargain with them, because you never know unless you ask. There are also a few companies out there that offer a "canned" commercial that all they have to do is insert your company name.

For the most part, however, advertising on TV and radio is not a way to market your business. If you are strictly after name recognition and have a marketing budget that allows you to regularly spend for advertising then you may get the results you are after. However, most people advertise because they need more business NOW, not six-months or a year from now.

Since TV and radio requires a great deal of repetitive advertising and therefore a large budget to be successful, the written media is the best "bang for the buck". Again, remember that print also comes with the same business needs. These companies need to fill the space in their publications by both advertising and articles. You may be able to suggest they write an article about you and your business, especially if you are a paid advertisers.

There is a wide-range of publications that are suitable for a PI to advertise in and some of these include the following:

- <u>Local newspapers.</u> Although this definitely works, it can be very expensive. To place a business card advertisement in San Antonio, Dallas, Houston or a similar market, you will pay $1,200-$2,800 per week. The way around this is to put a small personal advertisement in the classified under "personals." I have seen other investigators do this and one in particular has had the same advertisement for a year. This tells me they are getting some business out of it or they wouldn't keep running it.

- <u>Business Journals.</u> In most areas, there is a journal similar to the San Antonio Business Journal. You can place a business card size advertisement in these for $50-$75 per week. I have a lot of people comment about seeing the advertisement as well as getting clients from it. You can also run a quarter-page advertisement for $400-$500 per issue.

- <u>University & College Newspapers.</u> If you are near any colleges or universities, try advertising in their newspapers. I picked up a corporate account one time because a student took the paper home and his dad read it and saw my advertisement. Be ready, however, for a lot of calls from students inquiring about a job.

- <u>Military Base Newspapers.</u> In many areas, there are military bases. In San Antonio, for instance, we have five bases. Each has their own newspaper. A typical cost for placing a business card advertisement is $30-50 per week.

- <u>Free newspapers.</u> Many areas have something similar to the North side Recorder, Northwest Recorder or some other name for a free newspaper. Many of these are thrown on residential yards and placed in stands at stores. A lot of people read these and the cost to place a business card size advertisement runs from $30-50 per week.

More aggressive print advertising is available as well that also more specifically targets a given market. If you are looking at insurance or law firm cases, there are publications that focus on this market. Some of these include:

- <u>Insurance Claims</u> Major cities usually have claims adjusters that work for a particular insurance company and are stationed geographically throughout the country to handle claims in the area, state or region. You have to advertise in the publication to obtain a copy but it is a great marketing tool. The directory lists each insurance company as well as each insurance adjuster by name. It is much easier to get through the switchboard if you have a name to ask for when calling. Just as important, the directory will list what types of claims the adjuster handles such as automobile claims, property claims, liability, etc. To advertise in one of these directories you generally have to pay a yearly fee and this may range from $1500 to $2500.

- <u>Bar Journals</u> Like the insurance claims directories many larger cities will have local magazines for lawyers. There are also state and national journals but these are out of the price range for most investigators. The local bar journal has information about cases, continuing education and a host of other information geared towards attorneys. You can place a quarter page advertisement that ranges from $500 to $1500 per month.

- <u>Medical Journals</u> Much like the preceding journals mentioned, medical journals may be an area where you can place an ad but you certainly need to do your homework and define what services to offer.

- <u>Transportation Journals</u> There are a host of journals directed at the various types of transportation functions including 18-wheelers, taxi-cabs, buses, trains and related providers. Again, if this is a market that you have set out to conquer, then these would be journals to consider.

There are advertisements that work and there are those that don't. When you are scanning through the classified advertisements and you see the work

"Sex" or "Make $100,000" you automatically zoom in on that. Likewise, your advertisement should have the same kind of "draw" or appeal. Just because the media says that it will cost so much to place a "business card" advertisement, it doesn't mean that you have to use your business card. It simply means that the size of the advertisement will be the size of a business card. One of the best advertisements I have ever used was one that had two eyes and the words, "spouse check" with them. Target your advertisement to the particular market that you are wanting to obtain new business. For instance, if you are placing in advertisement in one of the free newspapers, you probably will be seeking domestic related cases. If placing an advertisement in a business journal, you will probably want to target corporate investigations.

Some of the various advertisements I have used over the years included:

*Reminder that all materials herein are copyrighted and cannot be used without the express written authorization of Kelly E. Riddle.

KELMAR
ASSOCIATES

Kelly Riddle, Owner
Chosen #1 PI in the U.S.
All Types of Investigations

Surveillance
Backgrounds Checks
Pre-Employment
De-Bugging
Security Consulting
Insurance
Investigations

FREE CONSULTATIONS
Credit Cards Accepted
www.kelmarpi.com
C-05785
2553 Jackson-Keller #200
San Antonio, TX 78230

342-0509

ANATOMY OF AN AD

- Company Name
- Company Logo
- Company Address
- Phone Number
- PI License
- Types of Services
- Eye Candy

You have to supply the key elements in an ad that (1) draws them to your ad (2) tells them what you are offering and (3) tells them how to contact you.

*Note: You want the most important information to stand out such as how to contact you (phone number and website). Most licensing agencies in each state require your agency license number to also be on all advertisements.

KELLY RIDDLE-Owner
*Author Of 9 Best Selling Books
Chosen #1 P.I. In The U.S. And One Of The
Top 25 P.I.s Of The Century
Agencies Nationwide
Television Appearances: Sally-Jesse Raphael/Dateline*

Former Law Enforcement Officer

- Surveillance
- Undercover
- Missing Persons
- Divorce
- Marital Misconduct
- Pre-Employment Checks
- Security
- De-Bugging
- Insurance Fraud
- State-Of-The-Art Technology

www.kelmarpi.com

LIC #A-05785

2553 Jackson-Keller Rd.

KELMAR & ASSOCIATES

342-0509

Surveillance . Preemployment Screening
All Types Of Investigations
#1 P.I. In The Nation!

The above is a billboard that I have utilized. All types of advertising can be used to get your name and brand in the public eye!

There are times when you will want to advertise at events or conferences or similar events. You should have a variety of floor banners, table banners and booth displays. Above Kelly E. Riddle is pictured in front of (1) RecordPros.net banner (2) RecordPros banner additional banner (3) Kelmar Investigations and (4) PI Institute of Education banner.

I have also advertised on all of the Delta Airlines flights in their on-board radio segments. A three-minute segment comprised of the announcer asking questions and a reply being given was taped and placed on all flights for two months. As in many types of advertising, the return on investment was difficult to measure on this type of advertisement.

Creating an image, or "branding" your corporate identity also requires the use of logos that present a professional look. Many private investigators have a tendency to use the magnifying glass, the silhouette of Sherlock Holmes or some other over-used cliché. I have also attempted to have a clean corporate look for all of my logos. I would recommend you have a professional graphic person or web designer create the image. You should ask them to provide the logos to you in regular and high-resolution formats as well as in different sizes. This will enable you to use them on websites, letterhead, business cards and in different orientations (vertical or horizontal).

As in all types of atmospheres, you should re-examine your corporate look every 5-7 years. In doing so, your logos and advertisements do not become old and outdated. You will continue to have a clean appeal and catch the potential client's attention. Examples of the logos I have used include the following:

*Logo with website.

*Logo alone. Note change in color from green on the left to blue, etc. The previous colors were cutting edge and a trend that also dated the logo. As with furniture, clothing, and similar items, a more conservative look that will pass the time-test may be a better way to go if you do not want to change often.

Old Logo for PI School

New Logo for PI Institute

The important thing is to advertise on a regular basis. That doesn't necessarily mean every week, every two weeks or once a month. What it does mean is that you should keep your name out there on a regular basis. At any given time, I am advertising in 10-15 different ways. Where I may miss someone in one type of advertisement, I may get in front of him or her in another.

FINDING YOUR NICHE
Chapter Three

"First we thought the PC was a calculator. Then we found out how to turn numbers into letters with ASCII - and we thought it was a typewriter. Then we discovered graphics, and we thought it was a television. With the World Wide Web, we've realized it's a brochure."[26] Through the use of the internet, a pimple-faced teenager can appear to be the biggest and the best thing going. At some point you have to see what is behind the smoke and mirrors and figure out what will be sustainable. "Your decision not to join the crowd may be what God is waiting for to grant you revelation on how to deliver your family, your country, business, profession or even your church!"[27] It may be that you are spreading your efforts to wide and it is time to re-focus.

You have seen doctors and lawyers specialize in a particular area of expertise. Likewise, the private investigation industry is seeing a trend towards specialization as well. For the most part, no PI can be financially productive working only one type of case. However, if you specialize in surveillance, you can do domestic related surveillance, insurance related surveillance, corporate surveillance and the like. All surveillance has the same underlying fundamentals. Just because you specialize in surveillance doesn't mean that you can't do hidden asset searches, missing persons, medical malpractice or whatever else comes along. What it means is that you should <u>primarily</u> be known for one special service.

When marketing yourself to a potential client, it is always good already know the answers to the typical questions they will ask. One that is at the top includes, "what makes you different from all the other PI's out there?" You have to find your niche and use it to your advantage in your marketing. Some of us are fortunate enough to have a ready-made niche created for us. When I left the police department, I went to work for two insurance companies. One was known as the training ground for new adjusters because they didn't pay very well but it was a good place to start. I got to know a lot of adjusters who came and went to

---

[26] Douglas Adams
[27] Jaachynma N.E. Agu, *The Prince and the Pauper*

greener pastures. Since I already knew them personally, I went straight to this ready-made market when I started my own business. By that time, they had scattered throughout the different insurance companies. This gave me a foothold within a lot of different insurance companies and this obviously became my number one market. Based on this the question is, "what background do you have that you can build into a niche?"

Part of being known for a specific area of expertise involves writing articles and books on the subject, as well as speaking on that topic. Building a niche is just like marketing any other product and you have to market yourself in that fashion.

From a strictly business perspective, you should not place all your "eggs in the same basket" even if you do have a ready-made niche. There are outside factors that may adversely affect you or your niche market and will leave you struggling if not prepared.

As an example, when I started my business in the late 1980's, worker's compensation fraud was "the ticket" for plaintiff attorneys and for investigators. Even though the State of Texas created Texas Employers Insurance Association as the original insurance company to handle these types of claims, they ended up filing for bankruptcy protection and eventually went out of business. During the same climate, the legislature passed a tort reform that severely limited any negotiation of insurance benefits related to worker's compensation claims. It was not unusual for an insurance adjuster to call and ask me to come by and discuss a file and while there, other adjusters would hear my voice and call me over. I often walked out with 5-10 new cases and it was truly the hey-day of worker's compensation investigations.

Almost overnight, the whole climate changed and plaintiff attorneys were limited in the amount of fees they could get on a case. Since there were fewer mediations and lawsuits, there were also fewer cases to investigate. I was forced to find another way to generate income and cases. It is often said that necessity is the mother of invention. In this case, I have investigators and their families that depended on the income.

Nursing home abuse investigations became the next big source of income and it was not unusual for a plaintiff's attorney to pay us $50,000 - $70,000 per investigation. The attorneys would also spend thousands of dollars bringing in medical experts, nursing home experts and ultimately would spend $200,000 to $300,000 on all of the "team." The attorneys I worked for would consistently have cases where the award was $20 - $50 million dollars. I was one of the first private investigators to conduct these types of investigations and was the first to write a book on the subject. In some states, as well as Texas, the move for "lawsuit abuse reform" began to catch on. Another change in the law pertaining to the amount of money a plaintiff could be awarded caused most of the big nursing home abuse attorneys to move out of state. They simply could not spend the amount of money working up a case for awards that were dramatically limited.

Once again, the necessity to change became apparent. I began to heavily market corporate America. Companies employee of services due to internal thefts, threats from terminated employees, sexual harassment, violation of no-compete agreements and a host of other reasons. Learning from the past, I continued to seek new ways to generate a consistent work flow.

The next move was into the pre-employment background screening sector of corporate America. Through our on-line secure system, our clients log in and run backgrounds that are Fair Credit Reporting Act compliant. We bid on contracts and have dramatically increased this segment of our business. Through our system, other private investigators can also use RecordPros.net to generate more income. We set the PI up as the master account and all of the companies they bring in are a sub-account of their account. They can log in at any time and see how many backgrounds their clients are running. At the end of the month, we send the PI an invoice. They mark it up and send to their clients.

If you take the time to look around, you will note that 18-wheeler and cargo is the number one economy worldwide. We were able to identify those insurance companies that specialize in just these types of policies. Once we started getting cases from these insurance companies, many of the transportation companies began to call us directly. These companies often have high deductibles and therefore contract with us in hopes of regaining the equipment or cargo fairly quickly.

While creating a new niche in each of these areas, we also got involved in the burglar alarm business. We charged for the installation and service of the equipment as well as the monthly monitoring fees. Through the years we increased the number of accounts to a level that allowed this part of the company to be spun off and sold in April of 2013.

Often clients also want Closed Circuit TV (CCTV) systems installed in their house or business when they install burglar alarm systems. We also got into this area of the business and still install these types of systems.

Training has been a service that we started early in the business by offering classes to other PI's and those interested in getting into the profession. Like many businesses affected by the internet, we moved our classroom instruction on-line at the PIinstitute.com.

When Kelmar started in 1989, we performed 100% insurance investigations. Because of the nature of business, we were forced to diversify the types of services. This has enabled us to continue to grow each year and not to have as much of the roller-coaster business cycles. Currently, insurance investigations only account for approximately 25% of our business services.

Developing a niche is important but that also gives a sense of a single path. A niche should be developed, but in conjunction with other fundamental services. Accordingly diversify is, "to produce or sell more kinds of products; to increase the variety of goods or services produced or offered by (someone or something)."[28] A niche should be a target market that few others know about or have the expertise to develop. All of the above mentioned niche markets that I developed was done while still relying on infidelity investigations, missing person investigations, general backgrounds and related services.

A niche market will only be there for a limited time by very nature. The goal is to identify a segment of society or business that is untapped and develop a method for meeting their needs. "There is, however, a con to niche marketing. The limitation lies in the very nature of niche marketing, to wit, you are focusing

---

[28] Merriam-Webster Dictionary

on a subsection of the overall market. Even if you become the biggest fish in the pond, you are still in a pond."[29] At some point others will take notice and attempt to move in on the turf you had dominated. Legislation may cause the market to disappear or be dramatically reduced.

A study of the market may need to be conducted before setting out on a niche market path. As an example of niche marketing, a study of the industry related to farmers in a particular community was conducted in an attempt to identify niche markets for them to service.[30] They had to look at the various outlets for their products as well as expenses related to producing the additional product for the new market.

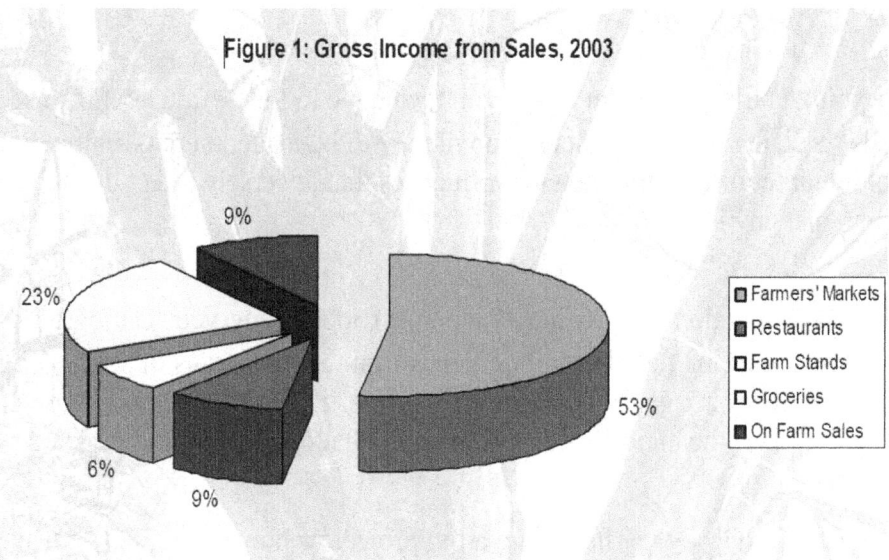

---

[29] www.marketingtitan.com

[30] http://www.ruralroots.org/Programs/nwdirect/casestudies

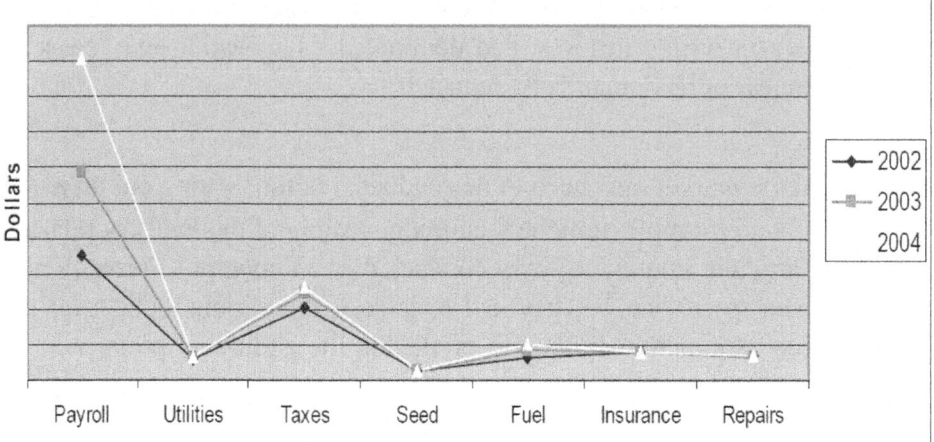

Figure 3: Expenses by Year, 2002-2004

Once you identify a potential niche, you then have to fully evaluate this to see if no one is servicing it because there is no money to be made, there is simply not enough of a market or there are outside influences that adversely affect the ability to operate in that environment.

Part of the evaluation process may encompass identifying your demographic market. If you are trying to help senior citizens from being victims of scams, you need to determine what age groups are most at risk, if there is a certain type of scam that takes place the majority of time and why that demographic is targeted.

Before jumping head over heels into a big project, you may want to test drive your product against the market. This will tell you if your product, approach to marketing, general presentation or information needs to be tweaked. You should also develop a theme for this new product such as low pricing, long-term personal protection, asset protection of other themes that make the service stand out in a crowd.

The pros far out-weigh the cons as niches are concerned. While you may limit yourself to a relatively small market, it is much easier to become dominant in it at nominal expense. Because the market is smaller, this gives you the opportunity to develop more of a bond with customers as well as develop customer loyalty.

THE POWER OF THE WRITTEN WORD
Chapter Four

Writing is a tool within itself and can be an asset or a hindrance. I can tell you that I have found it to be an asset. When I finished my very first book, I sent a free copy to some of the companies that I had been trying to get a foothold in. <u>They started calling me</u> and in their eyes, I was suddenly "somebody". The book propelled me (in their eyes) into a true expert and professional just because I had written a book. I still did the same work at the same rate as before, but it just goes to show you how much of an effect the written word can have on someone else.

"Behold the power of the written word - the most powerful invention of mankind. Entire civilizations have been forgotten because they did not master the written word. Entire religions have risen and fallen depending on how well they recorded and preserved their beliefs in writing.

It was the written word, in the form of books, newspapers and pamphlets that declared the fundamental belief that slavery was immoral, and should be illegal. It was the written words scribbled on a piece paper by which Abraham Lincoln honored the brave soldiers on both sides of the Battle of Gettysburg:

That we here highly resolve that these dead shall not have died in vain - that this nation, under God, shall have a new birth of freedom - and that government of the people, by the people, for the people, shall not perish from the earth.

It was the written words of the Thirteenth Amendment that actually ended slavery.

It was the written word that spread Christianity across the entire globe.

In fact, every religion that exists today stands as a testament to its power.

Reputations of the greatest leaders in the world have been both created and destroyed by it."[31]

The problem with the written word is that it has to be fresh. If you are discussing a topic that someone else has already discussed, you have to find a new angle or go into greater detail. Time is a valuable commodity and people will not "stay with you" if they are not being entertained in some form or fashion. As a writer, it is hard to stay fresh and exciting. As a speaker, it is even more difficult. If you said something you wished you hadn't, it's too late, whereas in writing, you can go back and edit. There are several issues that need to be addressed when dealing with writing. Number one, writing isn't everything. Presentation is just as important. The item has to be appealing to the eye to begin with so that it will attract the person to the writing. As an example, we will discuss the following:

> Business Cards. I intentionally used a generic business card when I first started off for several reasons. First, I was dealing with insurance personnel. It used to be that the average age of a claims adjuster was in their late 40's and older. This group is generally more conservative and less flashy. I wanted to be professional without coming across as arrogant. However, as time has gone on, I have become much more diversified and the average age of an insurance adjuster has dropped. I intentionally left off any indication that I was a private investigator in any way. My card simply had "Kelmar and Associates" on them. This is because I never knew when I might be in a bind on an investigation and be forced to give out a business card. If it didn't say what I did, it may have not been a problem. Secondly, when I first opened the company, we did insurance damage appraisals as well as investigations for insurance companies. I could use the same business card for all occasions.

The business card needs to have basic information on it such as your company name, your name and title, telephone numbers and your address. It has now become just as important to include your e-mail address, web site and/cell number on the card.

As business grew, we diversified and graphics have become much more utilized. We transitioned into business cards that make a statement and stick

---

[31] Dan Castro http://EzineArticles.com/4870128

out. Cards with some type of logo tend to stick in people's minds better. However, I have found that if you choose a "cheesy" logo, it can work the opposite.

Originally I used a light blue card stock with dark blue font. The color of the card and the color of the print on the card are a major issue. Think about this, when you drop a business card into a bowl for a drawing, the ones that stick out are those that are not white. Most cards are white and therefore your card should be anything but white. The business card can be a subtle reminder that they need to send you some business, even when they are flipping through their business card Rolodex for someone totally unrelated.

My original business card was on light blue linen with dark blue writing. An example of my business card is as follows:

Kelmar and Associates, Inc.
Private Investigations (Lic.# A-05785)

<u>Kelly E. Riddle, President</u>

2553 Jackson Keller, Suite 200
San Antonio, Texas 78230

Office: (210) 342-0509   Fax: (210) 342-0731
E-mail: kelmar@stic.net   Pager: 231-9847
1997-98 NAIS PI of the Year/Book of the Year

Like everything else, my business cards have transitioned:

KELMAR & ASSOCIATES HAS A PRESTIGIOUS TRACK RECORD OF PROVIDING QUALITY SERVICES INCLUDING:

Investigations: www.kelmarpi.com
Internet Background Services: www.RecordPros.net
PI Training: www.PIinstitute.com
PI Equipment: www.SpyTekSanAntonio.com

• Chosen #1 PI in the U.S. by PI Magazine • PI of the Year by NAIS • One of the Top 25 PI's of the 20th Century • Author of 10 Books • Featured on Dateline, Montel, Fox and More

"Relentless Pursuit of Excellence"

KELMAR
ASSOCIATES

KELLY E. RIDDLE
President

KELMAR & ASSOCIATES HAS A PRESTIGIOUS TRACK RECORD OF PROVIDING QUALITY INVESTIGATIONS INCLUDING:

- BACKGROUND INVESTIGATIONS
- PRE-EMPLOYMENT EVALUATIONS
- COMPUTER INVESTIGATIONS
- INSURANCE INVESTIGATIONS
- FINANCIAL LOSS CASES
- SECURITY ASSESSMENTS
- BUG SWEEPS - COUNTER MEASURES
- WITNESS LOCATION/SKIP TRACE
- PRODUCT LIABILITY CASES
- SURVEILLANCE VIDEO
- VULNERABILITY ASSESSMENTS
- CHILD CUSTODY CASES
- CRIMINAL HISTORY SEARCHES
- DOMESTIC CASES
- ALARM MONITORING
- CCTV SYSTEMS
- HIDDEN ASSET SEARCHES
- TRADEMARK INFRINGEMENTS
- MEDICAL MALPRACTICE CASES
- NURSING HOME ABUSE CASES
- RECORD SEARCHES
- WORKER'S COMP. CASES

PRIVATE INVESTIGATIONS & SECURITY CONSULTING

2553 Jackson Keller Rd., Suite 200
San Antonio, TX 78230
Phone: (210) 342-0509
Fax: (210) 342-0731
License #: C-05785
E-Mail: kelmar@kelmarpi.com
Web Site: www.kelmarpi.com

(210) 342-0509
(888) 873-1714

Current business card:

KELLY RIDDLE
PRESIDENT

Corporate Headquarters:
2553 Jackson Keller, Ste. 200
San Antonio, Texas 78230
License #: C-05785

Office: 210.342.0509
Fax: 210.342.0731
Email: Kelly@KelmarGlobal.com
Web: www.KelmarGlobal.com

A good business card has to be appealing, which includes a nice logo. You also need to get the basic information on the card which is primarily how to contact you (phone, address, email and website). *Remember your PI license has to be included in advertising according to state regulations.

➢ Newsletters. A company newsletter tells a lot about the company and therefore, presentation is once again important. I have clients that will call me up and will be upset if they didn't get a newsletter. They look forward to them and want them. This is because I try to make them entertaining and fun while being informative. Part of this is through the presentation. I always choose a pastel color for the paper like green, yellow, red or blue. They have to be pastel because they are still light enough that the writing can be easily read. By choosing a color like this, my clients know exactly what it is when they see it. Secondly, when a stack of mail is lying on their desk, they can pick my newsletter out of the stack. The color acts as a magnet for their eyes to attract to. In my newsletters, I try to convey a couple of cases that they will find interesting. Everyone likes to hear a PI's war-stories, and of course, you leave out identifying information and make it somewhat generic. I also try to include a "Did You Know" column that has statistics and interesting short facts. Most people that read the newsletter will only read something that is a couple of paragraphs long and nothing that is more than a couple of pages in length. They are busy and just don't have the time for anything much longer.

Besides having a newsletter and choosing the right colors, consistency is an important issue. My clients know that I send a newsletter out every-other month. They can count on seeing it and look forward to it. It is important that you develop one that is sent often enough to keep your name in front of them, while at the same time, not being too frequent. Cost is a factor as well, and every time you print newsletters and mail them, it cost money in addition to your time. Using a bulk mail permit from the post office to help cut down on the cost of mailing may be beneficial. However, I found that the money you save on mailing is given up in the amount of time you have to spend at the post office getting everything done just right for them to accept it as bulk mail. In addition to mailing newsletters to your current clients, you should add potential clients to your mailing list. This will help to create potential business through name recognition.

Like everything else that has gone the way of the internet, so have the traditional newsletter. There are those that still find it refreshing to get something tangible in their hands. Others prefer the newsletter in an email format. A word of caution should be given here. If you choose to use an email version, make sure that it does not come from your primary email address as most likely someone will report it as spam. Once this happens, you will not be able to send (and in some instances receive) emails until you contact all the major search engines and get the issue resolved.

To avoid your email getting on the blacklist for spam, you can either use a cloud type email (Yahoo, Gmail, etc.) or you can pay a service to do this on your behalf. There are companies that put your information into a template type of email and send them embedded within an email. This limits the size of the newsletter and becomes more of an "In the News" source of information. You may also post it to your website and then simply send an email announcing that a current newsletter is available on your website. Like junk mail, newsletters sent by email are becoming a part of the massive amount of emails that people get each day.

➢ Brochure. I have heard many PI's say that they don't have a brochure because things keep changing and they would have to re-print all the time.

Instead, they use regular legal size paper and present this as their marketing material. I tend to use both. My brochure has pretty generic information that most PI's have in their brochures such as the type of services they offer. I take my brochure further and supplement it with additional information on legal paper that I can customize to the particular client. Brochures are something that everyone asks for and is a good icebreaker when you get in front of a prospective client. They do represent a certain financial outlay and should be created with this in mind.

My original brochure was done using "card stock" for my brochure cover. This is paper that is heavier than normal paper and is designed for business cards. I choose a "blue marble" design that looked like a marble design, but in blue highlights. I then choose a matching pastel blue paper for the inside pages. With each printing, I alternated between blue and gray colors for my cover and paper. In my brochure, I have the following categories:

A) Introduction
B) Investigative Services
C) Expertise
D) Computer Investigations
E) Membership
F) Invoice Structure
G) Seminars
H) The PI Institute of Education
I) Geographic Services
J) Kelmar and Associates At Work
K) Books and Products
L) Professional Biography and
M) Contacting Kelmar and Associates

The introduction tells the reader who we are and what we do. My introduction is as follows:

INTRODUCTION

Kelmar and Associates is a professional private investigative company designed to provide the business community with the additional resources necessary to compete in their industry. Our mission is to fulfill the client's goals utilizing the most effective and state-of-the-art methods available. Kelmar & Associates recognizes that our clients are operating in an ever-changing business environment that requires adaptation and aggressive results.

Kelmar and Associates offers a comprehensive range of professional services designed to assist our clients in reducing exposure to loss or in making informed, problem solving decisions.

The clientele of Kelmar and Associates include the leaders in the insurance industry, established law firms, airlines, retail businesses, gas and oil companies, municipalities, self-insured's and governmental agencies.

The company was incorporated in 1989 and has established themselves as a leader in the private investigation industry. We invite you to explore our services and hope that we can develop a close working relationship with you.

The next area in my brochure introduces the reader to our investigative services. My brochure in this area is as follows:

INVESTIGATIVE SERVICES

Kelmar and Associates has developed expertise in specific areas, however we exceed standards in all types of cases. Our ability to obtain confidential and discreet information for the client is imperative. While Kelmar and Associates maintains offices in Texas, their extensive resources allow successful retrieval of records and information worldwide.

Kelmar and Associates is designed to assist our client's specific needs in:

- Background Investigations
- Child Custody Cases
- Civil History Searches
- Computer Investigations
- Criminal History Searches
- Domestic Related Cases

- Due Diligence Searches
- Financial Loss
- General Liability Investigations
- General Security Assessments
- Hidden Assets Investigations
- Legal Support/Testimony
- Location of Witnesses/Skip Traces
- Medical Malpractice Cases
- Nursing Home Abuse Cases
- Pre-Employment Evaluations
- Product Liability Cases
- Record Searches/Retrieval
- Surveillance
- Video Documentation
- Vulnerability Assessments
- Worker's Compensation Cases

The next area in my brochure is the area of expertise. If you have qualifications like these, you need to promote them. The area of my brochure that deals with this topic is as follows:

EXPERTISE

Kelmar and Associates has a proven track record of providing quality investigations of all types. Specific areas of expertise have developed which include:

- Physical Surveillance: Mr. Riddle has been designated an expert in this area by N.A.I.S.

- Insurance Investigations: Mr. Riddle has been designated an expert in this area by N.A.I.S.

- Nursing Home Abuse: Mr. Riddle has developed expertise and success in these types of investigations and is the author of "Investigating Nursing Home Abuse."

- General Backgrounds: Mr. Riddle has developed expertise and success in these types of cases and is the author of "Private Investigating Made Easy."

- Computer Related Investigations: Through the affiliation with Mr. Joseph Seanor, expertise has been developed in this area of specialization.

Because computer investigations are such a hot topic and will continue to be a hot topic, I have included information about our capabilities in this area. I will skip this information due to certain agreements with other parties.

Membership in other organizations is important to demonstrate as it shows you are involved in your profession. My brochure lists the following information in this area;

MEMBERSHIP

- Association of Christian Investigators (ACI) was founded by Kelly E. Riddle and chosen as the Association of the Year (1996-97) by NAIS.
- National Association of Investigative Specialists (NAIS)
- Texas Association of Licensed Investigators (TALI)
- National Association of Investigative Specialists
- Global Investigators Network
- Louisiana Association of Private Investigators
- Investigators On-Line Network
- American Society of Industrial Security (ASIS)
- San Antonio Claims Association
- Corpus Christi Claims Association
- Austin Claims Association
- Texas Board of Private Investigators

Through these associations, Kelmar and Associations maintains the highest training standards and has access to investigators worldwide.

The next topic in my brochure is our invoice structure that outlines what our hourly rate is, as well as related expenses. After that comes the topic of "seminars" and the brochure information we have is as follows:

SEMINARS

Kelmar and Associates have been certified by the Texas Department of Insurance and the Texas Board of Private Investigators to provide Continuing Education Courses for adjusters and PI's. Mr. Riddle also provides paid-seminars for the general public. For more information, please contact our offices.

Through these associations, Kelmar and Associations maintains the highest training standards and has access to investigators worldwide.

The next topic in our brochure is "The PI Institute of Education," which is a school conducted by Kelly Riddle. This helps to further establish credibility to clients and our brochure reads as follows:

THE PI INSTITUTE OF EDUCATION

The PI Institute of Education was founded by Kelly E. Riddle to teach continuing education courses to PI's and insurance adjusters. In addition, courses are offered to the general public as a way of introducing them to the PI industry. Courses are taught in 2, 8 and 16-hour segments and include such topics as:

* Nursing Home Abuse Cases
* Using the Internet in Investigations
* Accident Scene Investigations
* Insurance Fraud Investigations
* Surveillance Techniques
* Hidden Asset Investigations
* Homicide Investigations
* Record Searches
* And more!

The next topic in our brochure deals with record searches and our ability to retrieve records worldwide. Our brochure on this subject reads as follows:

RECORD SEARCHES AVAILABLE

Kelmar and Associates have developed a proven and safe method for obtaining records. Our office is able to conduct record searches worldwide from our office and records available include:

- National Criminal History Check
- County/State Criminal History Check
- County/State Civil History Check
- Federal/State Penitentiary Search
- Federal Civil/Criminal/Bankruptcy
- Worker's Compensation Claims
- Driver's License History
- License Plate Registration
- Voter Registration Search
- Education Verification
- Boat Ownership Search
- Aircraft Ownership Search
- Liens & Judgments
- Lawsuit Search
- Social Security Identifier
- Corporate Ownership
- Sales Tax Information
- Assumed Name Records
- Real Property Ownership

Dossier Report which provides description, social security #, driver's license information, voter's registration, vehicles and boat/air- plane ownership, current and previous addresses, known relatives and known associates and more all in one report!

The next area of information in our brochure deals with the geographic areas that we deal in. Our brochure reads as follows on this topic:

GEOGRAPHIC SERVICES

Kelmar and Associates is based in San Antonio and investigations are conducted throughout the Texas from the San Antonio location. Record searches can be conducted from the San Antonio office anywhere in the continental United States. Cities included are Corpus Christi, Austin, Houston, Dallas, Victoria, Del Rio, Laredo, Waco, McAllen and the surrounding communities.

In addition, we have investigators in the following locations:

Domestic:

- Oklahoma
- California
- Louisiana
- New York
- Alabama
- Florida
- Virginia
- Georgia
- New Mexico
- Arizona
- Ohio
- Illinois
- Texas (Corporate)

International:

- Mexico
- Canada
- Europe
- England (London)
- Asia (Hong Kong)
- Middle East (Israel)
- Australia

The next topic that we elected to put into the brochure is "Kelmar and Associates at Work." This is designed to entice the reader into taking a close look at the brochure. Our brochure reads as follows in this area:

KELMAR AND ASSOCIATES "AT WORK"

Mexico--Going Undercover:

A client requested Kelmar and Associates to spend a week south of Cancun, Mexico trying to get close to a person and prove their general character. Our operatives were able to obtain video and audiotapes of the subject confessing to 19 felonies, offering the investigators drugs, explaining how they smuggled guns and dynamite into Mexico and how he had his truck "disappear" to collect insurance.

Domestic Surprise:

A client asked our investigators to determine if her spouse was cheating on her. The first afternoon we conducted surveillance, the subject was followed as he picked up his girlfriend and went to and abandoned house where he parked his truck behind the house. Kelmar and Associates entered the abandoned house and obtained video of the couple engaged in a compromising position. While uninstalling hidden cameras in the subject's house, investigators found a hidden compartment under the water bed containing 19 fully automatic rifles, 30 cases of ammunition, patches indicating he was a member of a militia, a gas mask and a stock-pile of bottled water & food.

Uncovering the Conflict:

A law firm representing a national trucking company requested Kelmar and Associates initiate an investigation to determine whether or not one of their executives was engaged in a conflict of interest. The investigation resulted in documentation revealing the subject operated his own trucking company as well as being involved in his employer's company. Through the use of professional surveillance techniques, Kelmar and Associates substantiated the conflict of interest by obtaining photographic documentation of the subject's own trucks pulling the client's trailers for his personal benefit.

The Injured Employee:

Kelmar and Associates initiated an investigation with reference to an alleged injury that an employee claimed occurred during employment. Kelmar and Associates uncovered information indicating the subject had been injured the evening before the alleged employment injury in a domestic argument. Surveillance also resulted in photographic documentation revealing the subject was actively employed while drawing worker's compensation benefits.

Cash Register Theft:

A client requested Kelmar and Associates to conduct an investigation in reference to an employee suspected of stealing money from a cash register. Kelmar and Associates placed a hidden video camera in a smoke detector above the register. The employee was observed breaking into and stealing money out of the register. The tape was featured on REAL-TV and the Montel William's Show.

Fraud:

Kelmar and Associates was asked to investigate the apparent embezzlement of more than $300,000 from a bank. After a complete analysis of the bank's records, it was determined that more than $250,000 had been incorrectly documented due to improper book-keeping procedures.

The Citation:

Kelmar and Associates was asked to locate a defendant in a lawsuit. Kelmar and Associates utilized their extensive sources to track the defendant to Australia, Greenland and across the United States before successfully locating and serving the citation on the defendant who had fled to a small community in Tennessee.

Computer Break-In:

A client believed their computer system was being compromised. Kelmar and Associates determined that the system had not been broken into through a modem. Hidden video cameras were located in wall clocks, smoke detectors, exit signs and other things and the company employee who was breaking into the computer was identified and the system secured.

Paraplegic:

Kelmar and Associates conducted surveillance on a man who had been sitting in a car when hit by a train. The subject was supposed to be a paraplegic. Our staff observed and obtained video of the subject playing baseball.

The preceding case examples demonstrate the extraordinary success of our assignments, which is a product of the determination and expertise developed by the staff of Kelmar and Associates.

The next topic that is listed in our brochure is the books and other products that we offer. This is as follows:

BOOKS AND PRODUCTS

Kelly E. Riddle is the author of or has produced the following products:

Books:

- Book: "Private Investigating Made Easy"

- Book: "To Serve & Protect: The True Story"

- Book: "The Art of Surveillance"

- Book: "Find Out Fast-The Instant Guide to Private Investigations"

- Book: "Investigating Nursing Home Abuse"

- Book: "The Internet Black Book"

Software:

- Software: "Internet on Demand" which provide access to more than a

100 different topics PI's use on the Internet to conduct investigations.

- Software: "Information on Demand" which provides office address and phone numbers for government agencies, courthouses and other sources used by PI's.

- Software: "The PI's Guide to Reports" which provides example reports, forms and other things useful to PI's.

Soon to be released:

- Book: "Exposed: True Cases of a PI"
- Book: "Insurance Investigations from A to Z"

The next topic in the brochure is Kelly Riddle's professional biography, followed by how to contact our offices. These topics are as follows:

PROFESSIONAL BIOGRAPHY

Kelly E. Riddle
Owner/President

Industry Experience: Mr. Riddle has more than 35 years of investigative experience and earned a Bachelor of Science degree in Criminal Justice from the University of North Alabama. He was chosen as the **"PI of the Year"** by the National Association of Investigative Specialists and the PI Magazine named Mr. Riddle as the **"#1 PI in the United States"**. He has been designated an expert in surveillance, insurance investigations, nursing home abuse and computer investigations. He was chosen as **"One of the Top 25 PI's of the 20th Century."** Kelly obtained his **Texas Certified Investigator** designation (less than 50 in TX.) Mr. Riddle is also the past **President (2010-2012) for TALI** - the Texas Association of Licensed Investigators (TALI); **Board of Directors (2007-2010) for TALI** as well as being on the Board of Directors for the **Freedom of Information Foundation of Texas**. Kelly is on the Public Relations committee for the **Council of International Investigators** and the Membership Chair for the San Antonio Chapter of ASIS. He is a Founding Board Member and Board Advisor for the non-profit organization "Can You Identify Me." Kelly was the recipient of the **2013 Hudgins-Sallee award**, the highest recognition presented by the Texas Association of Licensed Investigators.

Prior Law Enforcement Experience: Prior law enforcement experience includes being a member of the SWAT Team, a Training Officer, Emergency Medical Technician, Evidence Technician, Arson Investigator, Traffic Investigator and Breathalyzer operator.

Education: B.S. degree in Criminal Justice from the University of North Alabama.

Other Credentials: Mr. Riddle is the Founder and President of the **PI Institute of Education**, as well as the **Association of Christian Investigators** with more than 1000 members in the U.S. and 19 countries. Kelly is the Founder of the **Coalition of Association Leaders** comprised of past and present board members from state, national and international associations.

CONTACTING KELMAR AND ASSOCIATES

Kelmar and Associates has continued to grow steadily since their inception in 1989. The number of case assignments and the number of clients have almost doubled each year. Even with our growth and success, we realize that taking care of the customer is our first priority. If Kelmar and Associates can be of service, we invite you to contact our home office.

Kelly E. Riddle
President

Office: (210) 342-0509
Fax: (210) 342-0731
E-Mail: Info@KelmarGlobal.com

Please visit our web site at:
http://www.KelmarGlobal.com

The brochure is done in a size of an envelope so we simply have to stick it in an envelope and mail. In addition, it can be placed in your coat jacket easily. It should be noted, that our agency license is enclosed in the brochure, on our letterhead and on our business cards to further signify that the client is dealing with a professional.

As mentioned, this was my original brochure and over time this has evolved into several other brochures with the paper changing as well as the graphics. The size has remained the same but the weight of the paper has changed along with our using a more glossy finish. Like everything in marketing, you have to re-evaluate every 5-7 years and create an up-to-date look.

I would suggest that you hire a professional to assist in this endeavor. While I originally created all of our brochures and websites, keeping up with changes in software and market trends is a full time endeavor. It also takes away from what you should be concentrating on; making money through investigations.

The email should be provided to you by your designer in multiple formats that will allow you to email. Since the internet is such a prominent tool, you may find that emailing your brochure will be done more than providing a physical copy.

Front Cover of current brochure

> Letterhead. This is another area that should be looked at closely. The final report is the only way that the client has of judging you and your company. Once again, color is important. I often review files with adjusters and attorneys and as they start to flip through the file, they immediately go straight to my report because I use blue linen paper. It sticks out in a crowd of white paper and helps draw attention to me.

Like everything else, we have re-evaluated our letterhead over the years and changed from the blue linen to white. The choice of logos had a lot to do with this as our logos have changed over time. Some marketing experts will tell you to keep the same logo forever as it becomes a way of readily identifying your company. While that is true *if* you have the right logo that is time resistant, many times you can simply change some of the colors or the font to retrofit the logo.

As with everything else discussed, the letterhead should be easily adapted to the internet. Reports today are often emailed so you should make sure that your letterhead presents well on the internet as well. The majority of time things in print do not show as well as on the internet due to the availability of high resolution. Be that as it may, you should strive to be as consistent across the board as possible.

Once all these areas are taken care of, you then have to get down to the act of writing. This can be a chore or you may be blessed with the ability to write. I have always written and it comes easy for me. Our company brochures, articles, books and the like are done directly from my head. In some instances hiring a profession agency to do this for the PI may be money well spent. This is OK, but the money may be better used elsewhere. When you are at a convention or seminar, there are usually brochures laying on the tables for others to pick up. Do it and then see how others have used certain wording and layouts that appeal to you.

Writing information about yourself or your company is always difficult, but that is where the "creative writing" terminology applies. Each of us have talents, it is simply recognizing them as a talent.

ASSOCIATIONS
Chapter Five

There are a lot of different associations that you should consider getting involved in that are both in as well as outside the PI profession. There are various reasons for joining an association, but very few valid ones for not joining. I have been a guest speaker at more than 350 conferences, seminars and the like and in almost every one of these, I have heard the topic of "why I should join an association" come up. It is interesting that one of the key arguments against joining is that of money. Each association does cost money to join and to participate in the seminars. However, many overlook the fact that the association brings a sense of professionalism, education and industry support, which in turn, brings money back into our individual pockets. Obviously, there are some associations that are run in a first class manner and some that have internal problems. The logical train of thought is which PI agency doesn't have the same problems, be it on a smaller scale?

An association that conducts itself in a first-class manner has first-class expenses. If you are going to take the time away from your business to go to a seminar, you expect the most for your time and money. Likewise, the association can only provide this type of service if they have the support of their members. Many times, it comes down to sheer numbers. To obtain the better meeting spaces, food, vendor rooms and discounted hotel rooms, the association has to guarantee a certain number of attendees. If the number is not met, the association still has to pay based on the contracted numbers. This brings up the flip side of members that just "pop-in" without pre-registering. Unfortunately, the type of business that we are in does not provide for a lot of future planning. It is a fact that more than 80% of PI agencies are 1-2 person agencies. If you get a last minute case in, you may not be able to go to the seminars. However, knowing that all meals, refreshments, attendee packets and related items are based on pre-registrations, each member should strive to pre-register.

One of the next statements that I tend to hear about why someone shouldn't join an association is that it is made up of too many cliques. Name me one organization that doesn't have this problem. Often, these cliques are not something by design but are instead due to need. In any organization, there is a handful (usually 20-30%) that does all the work. Because of this, they are usually called part of the "clique." The other related issue is that of personalities. Some are more out-going than others are. At many of these seminars, I often observe some of the more reserved and quite type of people sitting by themselves or away from the crowd. There is nothing wrong with that, unless you are there to become more in tune with the organization. I sometimes seek out these people and engage them in conversation in an attempt to determine if they want to be left alone or if they are too reserved to mingle. We should all do our part to mingle more and stay less in our "cliques." In this way, we can assist the association and the members grow closer.

Many trade associations have polled their members to determine why they come to conventions and regional meetings. Greater than 70% say that it is for the networking. Anyone who has attended a conference can testify to the value of meeting other PI's face-to-face. Personally, if my agency needs to refer or sub-contract a case to another PI, I will go to the ones I have met before I seek out anyone else.

I hear a lot of investigators complain about having to obtain continuing education credits. I am of the opinion that we need MORE required continuing education. This opinion was formed for several reasons, one of which involved some friends that work as real estate appraisers. Three of these friends complained one year about how they had less work and how there were too many appraisers all of a sudden. The industry caught on and increased the required continuing education requirements. Before long, many of the part-timers dropped out and everyone who made a living at it was once again making money. To me, it is self-preservation. Additionally, it is a good marketing tool. When I talk to prospective clients, I remind them that we have to keep up-to-date on issues within our industry due to the continuing education requirements. The associations are a great source of this education, and generally, you can count on the quality of these seminars.

Other reasons I have found for joining an association include:

✓ If you don't, your competitor will. Anyone who is a member of an association usually prints the information on their marketing materials. This shows clients that you are involved in your profession and are probably up-to-date on training.

- ✓ The meetings provide a great opportunity to network with others in other parts of the state, nation or world that you may need to call upon for help. Likewise, those you meet may need assistance from you as well. This brings up another topic of those investigators who indicate they are afraid to be around other investigators because they may "steal my clients and my secrets." I hate to tell you, but there are no secrets in this business. You know who most of your competitor's clients are and they know your clients. For me, I intentionally try not to market clients of other investigators I know and respect.

- ✓ None of us have the time or resources to keep up-to-date on all the changes in technology, government issues, legal issues, employment situations and related topics. Associations provide the opportunity to catch up on these issues.

- ✓ Associations are a good source for lobbying to gain support for our industry. In addition, they are a good source of flexing our muscles whenever legislation is introduced that radically affects us. One such issue currently being dealt with involves closing public records. Without our associations going to bat for us, we may lose major battles such as this.

- ✓ Associations provide the perfect platform for you to get better known within the profession. All of us are not speakers or authors, but you can network and you can lend assistance in other areas.

- ✓ Many associations have a committee that actively pursues those investigators operating without a license and helps to bring them under the enforcement actions of the licensing bureau.

- ✓ Associations seek out discounts for their members on hotels, airfare, office supplies and a host of other items.

The bottom line is that most people get out of any organization just what they put in to it. If you are a complainer, how about you re-directing this energy and putting it to good use. If you feel that something really needs changing, get involved and change it. Overall, I can tell you that associations are beneficial and useful to each of us, as well as the industry itself.

To take it a step further, trade associations provide you with the ability to showcase yourself. You have the option of writing articles for their magazine or newsletter, to speak at some of the seminars, to assist on some of the committees and to just out-and-out network with others. Like the media, trade magazines need new, fresh and interesting articles to put in their publications. If you will take the time to research and write some articles, your name will become better known and you will be providing a service at the same time. Each publication also allows members to place a business card advertisement in each magazine and I would encourage you to do that as well.

Personally I have been on the Board of Directors for the Texas Association of Licensed Investigators for 5 years and then was President for 2 years. I have been on numerous committees within other organizations and will continue to assist my fellow PI's every chance I get.

In addition to being involved with the leadership in these associations, I also founded the Association of Christian Investigators (ACI) and the Council of Association Leaders (COAL). I started ACI in 1997 as a way to help bolster the integrity of our profession. I founded COAL in 2012 and any former or current member of a PI association Board of Directors can be a member. COAL is designed to help guide the PI profession, lend the wealth of wisdom to current association boards and lead the fight where required.

There are some great organizations out there that I would suggest you become a part of. Some of these include:

- Your state private investigation association such as TALI (Texas Association of Licensed Investigators), FAPI (Florida Association of Private Investigators), CALI (California Association of Licensed Investigators) and similar organizations. These will help give you more local publicity and network contacts.

- The National Association of Investigative Specialists (NAIS), based in Austin, Texas. They have a tremendous wealth of professional training books and sell equipment through the Spy Exchange and their Law mate brand.

- ION, which is an investigator's referral network, is based in Tempe, Arizona. You pay a monthly fee and any cases that require your skills and are in your geographic area are referred to you.

- The PI Magazine, a trade publication based in New Jersey, is worth subscribing to as you get a wealth of information.

- The American Society of Industrial Security (ASIS) also publishes a magazine and they have seminars throughout the year.

- The National Association of Legal Investigators (NALI) is a national organization that also provides seminars throughout the year.

Other organizations that are useful for PI's are as follows:

Association of Christian Investigators
http//www.A-C-I.org

National Association of Investigative Specialist
http://www.pimall.com/nais

Florida Licensing and Registration
http://fcn.state.fl.us

National Association of Security and Investigative Regulators
http://www.nasir.org

High Technology Crime Investigation Assoc.
http://htcia.org

Retail Loss Prevention Exchange
http://www.nji.com/u/danno/rlpx.html

Listing of PI Associations
http://www.pimall.com/nais/n.piaweb.html

The Terrorism Research Center
http://www.terrorism.com

Michigan Council of Private Investigators
http://ourworld.compuserve.com/homepages/mcpi/

National Association of Investigative Specialists
http://www.pimall.com/nais

Texas Association of Licensed Investigators
http://www.tali.org

How to join the PI Mailing List
http://www.pimall.com/private-eye/peinfo.html

France Detectives Associations
http://france-detectives.com/

American Society for Industrial Security
http://www.asisonline.org/

California Association of Licensed Investigators
http://www.cali-pi.org/

National Association of Legal Investigators
http://www.nali.com/

World Association of Detectives
http://www.wad.net/

Once you have the trade related organizations down, it is time to step out and test the associations that are not trade related. Some of these include the bar association and the claims associations. In most major cities, there will be a local association of attorneys and insurance adjusters. There are also state organizations for each as well. These are good sources for promoting yourself and your business. For each of these, you should determine where they meet each month. The associations usually hold their meetings once a month over lunch while a speaker provides a seminar that provides them with continuing education credits. It is a good idea to go to these lunches and let them get to know you. It is important to note that like anyone you meet for the first time, you may not walk away with new cases right away. This is a process of letting them get to know you and building trust in you before they make any assignments. Once you have been to at least six of their meetings, seek out the opportunity to be one of the speakers. This is a great time to show case yourself in a subtle way. In addition to attending and speaking at these associations, you can also place a business card advertisement in their newsletters. Most of these associations also have directories like the "San Antonio Claims Association Directory," or the "San Antonio Bar Association Directory." You can advertise in these and use them in marketing. If you do work primarily in the medical malpractice area, look through the bar journal and determine those lawyers that specialize in that area. You can then send them your marketing material and put them on your mailing list.

If you don't know how to find out about the journal or meetings for these associations, call an insurance claims office. Ask for a supervisor in the claims department and explain that you are trying to find out if they have a local association, how you can advertise in their publications, when and where they meet and similar information. They will more than likely be happy to assist you and you have also opened a door with that insurance company. You can do the same thing with attorneys, but you can ask for the office manager, a paralegal or the attorney if it is a small office.

You should seek out every opportunity to mingle with potential clients. Some of these include Rotary Clubs, Lions Clubs, Chamber of Commerce meetings, church events, sporting events and other similar opportunities. Make it a point to carry business cards on you. A missed opportunity is a missed dollar!

THE POWER OF THE SPOKEN WORD
Chapter Six

Just like the written word, the spoken word can be a valuable tool as well. All of the TV, radio and associations need <u>good</u> speakers who are interesting, entertaining and informative. Speaking in front of any group is difficult and it usually requires repetition for you to overcome the stage fright. There are several keys to being a good speaker. One of which is to not be obvious about promoting yourself or your services. No one likes to hear a person stand up for an hour and tell about how great they are. If you present yourself properly and have a good presentation, this will speak more about you and your company than any obvious information you could give.

Being a speaker that is interesting and entertaining can be difficult. However, one of the keys is to throw in some "war stories" at the right time. I know one PI that doesn't do anything but tell war stories, and that is going to the opposite extreme. It is good to use some of your case experiences to help demonstrate what you are trying to get across. In addition, war stories act as a "refresher" and keeps technical information from becoming boring. Of course, jokes are always good for transition and for keeping everyone entertained. The problem is that you have to keep the jokes up-to-date and be good at telling jokes. I typically don't use jokes because I know that I am not good at the delivery of a joke. Therefore, I make up for it in other information and variations in my seminars.

You should also keep in mind that you will have a wide variety of attendees who have a diverse background. As such, you may touch some nerves if you use cursing, crude jokes or anything considered less than uplifting. "When we put bits into the mouths of horses to make them obey us, we can turn the whole animal. Or take ships as an example. Although they are so large and are driven by strong winds, they are steered by a very small rudder wherever the pilot wants to go. Likewise, the tongue is a small part of the body, but it makes great boasts. Consider what a great forest is set on fire by a small spark. The tongue also is a fire, a world of evil among the parts of the body. It corrupts the whole person, sets the whole course of his life on fire, and is itself set on fire by hell."[32] As a speaker, you have the stage and the attention of everyone present. You have a duty to use the forum in a responsible manner. If you want to do nothing but tell jokes and war stories then I suggest you go to a comedy club or some other appropriate venue. As an instructor, your information should be both entertaining and enlightening.

One way to be entertaining is to use a power-point presentation with your lap top computer. Using this type of presentation is a talent in itself as you don't want attendees to spend all of their time reading. Graphics are a huge asset and having something visual helps to break up the constant staring at a speaker. In addition, a picture really is worth a thousand words and they can be a great asset in a speech if used at the right times. I recently conducted a seminar on nursing home abuse and used a power-point presentation with pictures of some of the bedsores and bruises that are common in these types of cases. Obviously, before I used any photographs, I went through the thought process of determining if they were *too* graphic. I didn't use many of these because I thought they may have been too much. During the seminar, I observed two people leave briefly and they both sought me out later to apologize. Both subjects indicated that the photographs were a bit more than they were ready for, but they enjoyed the presentation. The point is, the photographs did exactly what I had intended. The audience was astonished by what they saw and they were moved by this information. My goal was to deliver a seminar that they would not soon forget, that was entertaining and informative, but was not too disgusting. As I presented this seminar in future venues, I put a mark in the corner of the slide that preceded photographs. I announced at the start that this was my way of preparing the viewer for a photograph that they may not want to see and gave them the opportunity to look away.

The use of a PowerPoint presentation should be done to provide bullet points or topics of discussion. I use it primarily to jog my memory and provide tantalizing phrases or fragments. Again, it should not be something that requires a great deal of reading. If you fill the screen with too many words you will soon see your audience squinting and paying

---

[32] James 3:3-6 (Oxford NIV Bible)

more attention to the screen that to you.

Another key element in giving a seminar is to be informative. If you are a PI and are talking to other PI's, this can be difficult because you have some that are brand new in the business and some that have been at it for decades. The trick is to hit the happy medium where everyone feels entertained and leaves with the sense of having learned something new. When selecting topics, it is a good idea to have a look around and see what is hot at that moment. A few decades ago, no one was really too concerned with computers and the Internet and now it is one of the hotter topics.

I would encourage you to have someone video tape your presentations so that you can go back and critique yourself. This can be a hard thing to do but one that is absolutely essential. When I first started speaking, I discovered that I had a habit of speaking too fast. That was just the way I talked but one that needed to addressed. Being from Texas, I also noticed that I was using local terms like "you'll" and "you guys" when meaning both men and women. When I slowed my speaking tempo, this allowed me to be more precise in the words I used and could therefore clear up these issues.

You may also catch yourself doing other things that are distracting like walking from one side of the platform to the other too much. Because I always try to relate to my audience, I was one of the guilty ones. I soon learned that keeping close to the podium and the laptop was a way to reduce this wandering. Critiquing yourself is certainly not an easy thing to do but one that will make you a better presenter.

A good habit to get into is to insure there is a glass of water on the shelf under the podium or a nearby table. Speaking tends to dry you out and may cause you to become hoarse or to cough. I quickly learned that prior to speaking; drinking a warm cup of tea with honey was a way to relax vocal cords. If you spend much time in a hotel/convention setting, these tend to dry you out as well so I would encourage you to drink more water.

Another skill to learn, especially if you are doing any type of TV or radio interview, is to speak in "sound bites". These are sentences with pauses at appropriate times within the sentence or after the sentence. This allows the producer to edit and/or take sections out and use for affect or to dramatize a topic.

10 Tips for Public Speaking[33]

Feeling some nervousness before giving a speech is natural and even beneficial, but too much nervousness can be detrimental. Here are some proven tips on how to control your butterflies and give better presentations:

> **1. Know your material.** Pick a topic you are interested in. Know more about it than you include in your speech. Use humor, personal stories and conversational language – that way you won't easily forget what to say.
>
> **2. Practice. Practice. Practice!** Rehearse out loud with all equipment you plan on using. Revise as necessary. Work to control filler words; Practice, pause and breathe. Practice with a timer and allow time for the unexpected.
>
> **3. Know the audience.** Greet some of the audience members as they arrive. It's easier to speak to a group of friends than to strangers.
>
> **4. Know the room.** Arrive early, walk around the speaking area and practice using the microphone and any visual aids.
>
> **5. Relax.** Begin by addressing the audience. It buys you time and calms your nerves. Pause, smile and count to three before saying anything. ("One one-thousand, two one-thousand, three one-thousand. Pause. Begin.) Transform nervous energy into enthusiasm.
>
> **6. Visualize yourself giving your speech.** Imagine yourself speaking, your voice loud, clear and confident. Visualize the audience clapping – it will boost your confidence.

---
[33] Toastmasters.com

7. Realize that people want you to succeed. Audiences want you to be interesting, stimulating, informative and entertaining. They're rooting for you.

8. Don't apologize for any nervousness or problem – the audience probably never noticed it.

9. Concentrate on the message – not the medium. Focus your attention away from your own anxieties and concentrate on your message and your audience.

10. Gain experience. Mainly, your speech should represent *you* — as an authority and as a person. Experience builds confidence, which is the key to effective speaking. A Toastmasters club can provide the experience you need in a safe and friendly environment.

Besides talking to trade associations, there are a number of other places that you can give seminars that include:

♦ School District Community Education classes have been a good source for me in past years. I conducted five classes every semester at one of the school districts in San Antonio for five years. This is a good source for spreading my name and the mail-out announcing the classes being offered are sent throughout the city by the district and it doesn't cost me a penny. I usually have a full room and that means about 40 people who now know me and can spread my name. I also sell my books and products at the classes, so I have a direct source of financial gain each time. The school district only pays an instructor about $20 per class, but I do the seminars primarily for the free advertising and word of mouth.

♦ Summer School programs through elementary, junior high and high schools are another good source of gaining speaking experience as well as marketing yourself. One district has me teach elementary and junior high age students for three hours a day during a week session in the summer. I teach them some hands on stuff like how to take fingerprints, how to handle a crime scene and similar things. The kids love it, I get introduced to their parents for marketing and I get paid $500 per week.

- There are several clubs that hold monthly meetings during lunch and are always needing someone to speak. These include the Rotary Club, the Kiwanis Clubs, the Optimist Clubs and Chamber of Commerce groups. Each of these are made up primarily of business people that is the perfect market to get in front of for marketing.

- Colleges and Universities are another good venue for speaking engagements. If they have a criminal justice, business, law degree program or something similar, these should be targeted. Many of these will be good contacts and/or clients once they graduate.

Of course, speaking at these types of events take planning and time. You can't accept an invitation to speak and then not show up due to a case. That is tacky and does not do the profession or your business any good. It is hard to commit to something when you are the only one working in a company, but you have to stick to any commitment that you make.

Your personal appearance should be a definite consideration whenever you're speaking or marketing clients. Before I bought my former business partner out, we had a situation that exemplifies this topic. He always played one of the Apostles in a play at church every year and would grow a beard during the holidays to be more believable in the part. One day, he was called by one of the adjusters for a good client and asked to stop by their office. He picked up the new case and everything went fine. The next time I was in the client's office, the manager asked me to step into his office and he closed the door. The manager advised me that my partner had been in the office with no tie and a beard. He stated plainly, "If you want to keep doing work for us, make sure he is presentable next time." I explained the reasoning behind this and assured him that it would not happen again.

I once heard someone tell me that people want to be around successful people. The concept is true. No one likes to hang out with a looser. You should therefore dress and act successful, without appearing too successful. People tend to get jealous of others who are too successful, so you have to play a tight rope.

Part of appearing to be successful is dressing the part. I know one PI that always wears blue jeans, a T-shirt with the sleeves cut off and hair to his collar. He said that this was his gimmick and would tell clients that he could go where others couldn't. He may or may not be right, but I can tell you that I have heard some of his client's say repeatedly that he looks like a looser. I tell my clients that we have investigators of every age, sex and race on staff so that we can fit into most situations. They don't need to see this, as long as they know it is available. My mother was the first to tell me, "it's better to be over-dressed than under-dressed." She is absolutely right. If you show up in a suit and everyone else is in jeans, you can always take off your tie and jacket. However, if you show up in jeans and everyone else is wearing suits, you are going to wish you had changed. It is a simple fact, people would rather see and hear someone who is good looking and presents themselves nicely than someone who doesn't. You have to put the whole package together if you are going to go marketing and speaking. Remember that you have competition!

There are other reasons to learn good speaking habits and to develop this ability. One of these is for undercover operations. If you are used to speaking under pressure, you will perform better if involved in an undercover operation. In addition, if you are called upon to testify or give a deposition, you will already have overcome the fear of speaking in public. Another reason is for making cold calls while marketing. Believe me, this is not easy, but it is part of the job. When you call a potential client, they immediately begin to size you up based on your voice command and how confident you come across. I have some pat phrases that I use when making cold calls that always seem to work. Some of these include the following:

- Mr./Mrs. _____, thank you for taking my call. I will be brief because I know we are all busy. My name once again is _____ and I am the owner of _____ investigations. I have been conducting investigations for more than _____ years and somehow I have managed to not become acquainted with your company. I would really appreciate the opportunity to meet you and some of your staff and thought I might be able to drop off some breakfast tomorrow or take some of you to lunch. Can I set an appointment please?

- Mr./Mrs. _____, I was referred to you by another of my clients who thought that since I have done such a great job for them, I might be able to assist you and your company as well. I own _____ investigations and we have a reputation for delivering quality investigations at a fair price. I know that the investigative industry has been our own worst enemy in the past, but I can assure you that we are a professional company that has been in business for more than ____ years. Being in business for that long in any business speaks volumes in itself. I would like the opportunity to meet you and your staff in person and explain exactly why we have done so well and how we can help you. Do you have a few minutes tomorrow?

- Mr./Mrs. _____, my name is _____ and I have some special talents that I am sure you will agree could be of benefit to you and your staff. I have developed an area of expertise in _____ types of investigations. I know that you deal in these same types of cases and would therefore suggest that we spend a little time in person so I can demonstrate how we can be an asset to you.

Any marketing is not a valuable tool unless you track it and follow up. I personally keep a file on my desk that I log each call while marketing. This allows me to refresh my memory before calling people and also reminds me of the people I haven't called in some time. If I get told that the person I am calling is on vacation or out sick, I make a note of this. The next time I call them, I ask them how their vacation was or if everything is OK. This shows them that you care and puts you on a more personal level.

Learning how to speak effectively and taking advantage of all the opportunities available are important aspects for investigators. This is just like any other tool in our arsenal and we must strive to improve this ability daily.

CHARACTER IS EVERYTHING AND SO ARE RECORDS
Chapter Seven

A person's character and integrity is important to everyone. However, being a private investigator requires this to be exemplified even more. Your clients are counting on you as well as your employees and your family. If you shortchange yourself, it is going to affect each of these. I have had potential clients, attorneys and other PI's call and ask me to obtain illegal information. I had one attorney call me recently and said that he represented a lady who was filing for a divorce from her husband. He said that she felt certain he had some incriminating photographs in his desk and asked if I would break into his office and retrieve them. That is an obvious no-no, but what about those areas that are commonly labeled "gray" areas. Walking in the gray areas is dangerous, because you often can't tell when you have crossed into the illegal area. Once you have done it, there is no going back and it's too late.

I remember working for a nationwide investigation company before I opened my own company. The company had 26 offices and all information requests went through the home office. The information was retrieved and faxed to each office. I began to see information that I knew could not be legal to possess. One day they left the heading at the top that had the telephone number of where the information originated. I re-traced the number and figured out where it came from. Not long afterwards, the company went under and I started my own business. I received a call from the information source asking me to start using them. I politely declined and less than a year later, I read where the FBI and IRS had raided the information source. They arrested the information provider as well as people throughout the country in the IRS, Social Security Administration, law enforcement officers and others that had sold the information. Of course, they now had their computers which contained the customer database. There were PI's that were arrested for getting illegal information such as credit reports without a written authorization. This demonstrates exactly what I am talking about. A client starts to push you for more and more information and eventually you give in and do something stupid. After all, we are PI's and we are supposed to be able to get anything from anyone, right?

Whatever information you get that is not legal to have is a time bomb waiting to go off. To begin with, if it cost you $200 to get the information, the most you could charge is $600. I don't know about you, but it isn't worth going to jail, losing my license and my livelihood and missing my family for this. Once you get a reputation, good or bad, it stays with you. The PI profession once deserved the characterization that we had. A majority of PI's were ex-cops that got in trouble and got kicked off the department. They were alcoholics that slept in their offices and needed a bath. That is not true of today's investigators. Most are highly trained and skilled and the "job" is treated as a profession. In fact, a summary of the PI profession describes just the opposite.

According to the Bureau of Labor Statistics, in 2012 there were approximately 109,230 private investigators throughout the United States.[34] The starting average annual salary is $39,900 ($19.18 per hour) and the median salary is $74,300 ($35.72 per hour).

National estimates for this occupation:

Employment estimate and mean wage estimates for this occupation:

Employment (1)	Employment RSE (3)	Mean hourly wage	Mean annual wage (2)	Wage RSE (3)
109,230	0.5 %	$37.43	$77,860	0.4 %

Percentile wage estimates for this occupation:

Percentile	10%	25%	50% (Median)	75%	90%
Hourly Wage	$19.18	$25.16	$35.72	$47.57	$59.13
Annual Wage (2)	$39,900	$52,320	$74,300	$98,940	$122,990

However, these statistics from the Bureau of Labor Statistics is high suspect as it does not speak directly to *private investigators* as a standalone profession.

---

[34] http://www.bls.gov/oes/current/oes333021.htm

Their statistics (see below) deal with those listed as an investigator in university, hospitals, government and related jobs and are therefore not truly private investigators. A true private investigator does not work for a single employer. According to definition, a private investigator "is a person who can be hired by individuals or groups to undertake investigatory law services".[35]

Industries with the highest levels of employment in this occupation:

Industry	Employment (1)	Percent of industry employment	Hourly mean wage	Annual mean wage (2)
Local Government (OES Designation)	46,250	0.85	$31.06	$64,610
Federal Executive Branch (OES Designation)	43,450	2.13	$48.22	$100,290
State Government (OES Designation)	18,820	0.86	$28.11	$58,460
Postal Service	520	0.08	$43.07	$89,580
Colleges, Universities, and Professional Schools	100	0.00	$32.35	$67,280

Industries with the highest concentration of employment in this occupation:

Industry	Employment (1)	Percent of industry employment	Hourly mean wage	Annual mean wage (2)
Federal Executive Branch (OES Designation)	43,450	2.13	$48.22	$100,290
State Government (OES Designation)	18,820	0.86	$28.11	$58,460
Local Government (OES Designation)	46,250	0.85	$31.06	$64,610
Postal Service	520	0.08	$43.07	$89,580
Psychiatric and Substance Abuse Hospitals	60	0.02	$32.29	$67,160

Top paying industries for this occupation:

---

[35] http://en.wikipedia.org/wiki/Private_investigator

Industry	Employment (1)	Percent of industry employment	Hourly mean wage	Annual mean wage (2)
Federal Executive Branch (OES Designation)	43,450	2.13	$48.22	$100,290
Postal Service	520	0.08	$43.07	$89,580
Colleges, Universities, and Professional Schools	100	(7)	$32.35	$67,280
Psychiatric and Substance Abuse Hospitals	60	0.02	$32.29	$67,160
Local Government (OES Designation)	46,250	0.85	$31.06	$64,610

To be more industry specific, information from the Texas Association of Licensed Investigators[36] revealed the following statistics based on a 2011 survey of membership:

*Statistics based on the number of association members responding to survey.

What is your current age:

21-25	1.00%
26-30	1.75%
31-35	6.50%
36-40	8.25%
41-45	12.75%
46-50	17.25%
51-55	29.50%
56-60	13.25%
61-65	6.50%
66-70	3.25%
71-+	0.00%

---

[36] TALI – www.TALI.org

What is your *company's* gross income:

LESS THAN $50,000	28.57%
$50,000-75,000	3.57%
$75,100-100,000	14.29%
$100,1100-125,000	10.71%
$125,100-150,000	0.00%
$150,100-175,000	7.14%
$175,100-200.000	3.57%
200,100-250,000	3.57%
250,100-300,000	0.00%
300,100-350,000	10.71%
350,100-400,000	0.00%
400,100-500,000	0.00%
500,100-750,000	3.57%
750,100-1,000,000	7.14%
1,000,100-2,000,000	3.57%
2,000,000-3,000,000	0.00%
3,000,000-5,000,000	3.57%

How many investigators work for your agency or the agency you are employed by:

	1	48.15%
2		18.52%
3		11.11%
4		0.00%
5		7.41%
6		0.00%
7		0.00%

8	3.70%
9	0.00%
10 to 15	7.41%
16 to 20	0.00%
21 to 25	3.70%
26 or more	1.00%

What is the primary source of your income (case types):

Criminal Defense	8.63%
Personal Injury	7.91%
Domestic Matters (fidelity, custody, divorce, etc.)	9.35%
Criminal Prosecution	2.88%
Pre-employment	5.76%
Backgrounds	11.51%
Civil Cases	12.23%
Insurance Cases	9.35%
White Collar	4.32%
Adoptions	2.16%
Missing persons	3.60%
Interviews (witnesses, claimants, applicants, etc.)	10.79%
Personal Protection (Bodyguard)	2.16%
Security	2.88%
Technical Countermeasures	1.44%
Mystery Shopping services	0.00%
I do whatever walks in the door	3.60%
Mitigation issues	1.44%
I sale only and sub contract out the work	0.00%
I do only the items checked above	0.00%

How did you gain your experience:

Insurance industry investigations	7.32%
Prior local or state Law Enforcement experience	26.83%
Prior Legal related employment	7.32%
Banking, collections, lending experience	0.00%
Military experience	4.88%
Registered PI for another licensee	21.95%
Federal Law enforcement	14.63%
Federal Intelligence Agency experience	4.88%
Business experience	2.44%
Undercover experience	2.44%
Sales Experience	2.44%
Security primarily with some investigation	0.00%
Self-employed and got credit for my work	0.00%
Something else entirely	4.88%

How long have you been employed as a PI:

Less than 2 years	6.25%
2-5 Years	31.25%
6-10 Years	15.62%
11-15 Years	18.75%
16+ Years	28.12%

When you work as a PI it is:

My Only Job?	48.48%
My Post Retirement Job?	24.24%
My Part-time job?	6.06%
One of several businesses?	21.21%
Something to stay busy?	0.00%

This sheds some closer light on the job functions and performance of those actually involved in the profession and not subject to a random government poll of the non-PI related jobs.

TALI Summary

The summary of the Texas Association of Licensed Investigators poll indicates:

1) the average age of private investigators are middle-aged (41-60)

2) almost half of all PI agencies are 1 person operations (48.15%);

3) slightly more than 33% get their income from backgrounds and civil cases

A closer look finds the following statistics more closely in line with the actual field. According this information, a private investigator makes $36,000 to $86,000.[37]

---

[37] http://www.indeed.com/salary/Investigator.html

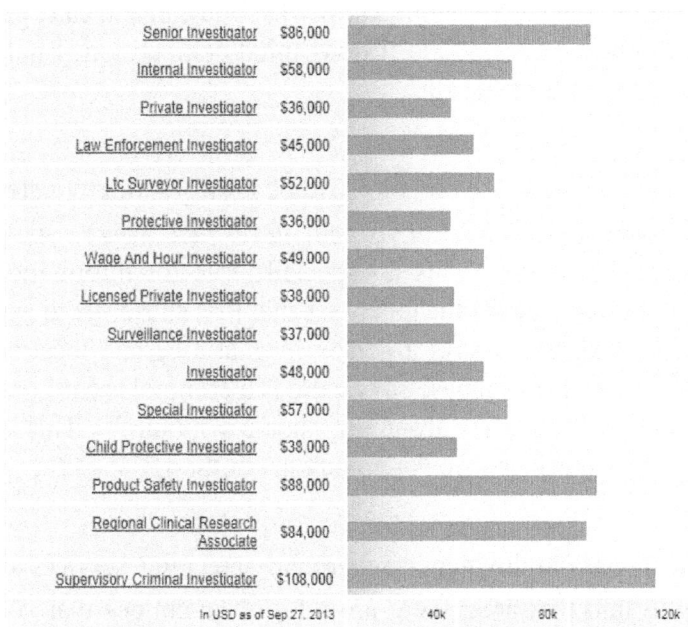

In a survey conducted by the PI Magazine, the survey results found that less than 16% of all male PIs are younger than 41. The majority group seems to be those male private investigators in the 41 - 50 year old bracket at 31%. However, the current survey results revealed that 52% of all male PI's are over 50 years of age, of which 22% are over 60. The PI Magazine also concluded the size of agencies as reported by PI's:

1 Person – 66%
2 People – 11% (owner plus one full-time employee)
3-5 Employees (full-time) 18%
6-10 Employees (full-time) 2%
11+ Employees (full-time) 3%

While this increased professionalism is good across the board, there still is the opportunity for PI's to drift into the illegal side, mostly out of ignorance. If they never worked for any other agency, they have one hand tied behind their back to begin with. Trying to learn how to run a business is tough. Trying to find out where to get legal information at the best price is another task. I get hundreds of brochures and emails in my office each year and each advertise what information they can obtain for you. If you don't know what you can and can't get legally, you can drift over into the illegal side. I don't mind competition; I only mind dumb competition because it hurts us all.

Information that is obtained in what you believe to be legally is often treated as the gospel. *Any information received is an unverified source until collaboration and verification is made.* This is especially true for information obtained off the internet. It is even true for the databases that PI's subscribe to and use every day. Just because a database says a person lives at a certain location doesn't make it so until verified. If a database says there is a criminal record or a lawsuit, you need to obtain the specifics from the "horse's mouth." This is usually the District Court Clerk for the particular county in question.

For those involved in pre-employment background screening services or may be anticipating getting into that area, there are a lot of landmines that you need to navigate. One resource for learning more about this is NAPBS[38]. According to their mission statement, "The National Association of Professional Background Screeners (NAPBS) exists to promote ethical business practices, compliance with the Fair Credit Reporting Act, equal employment opportunity and state consumer protection laws relating to the background screening profession. The NAPBS provides educational programs aimed at empowering members to better serve clients and to maintain standards of excellence in the background screening profession."

In a *very* simplified summary of requirements associated with pre-employment background checks, you most assuredly will first have to have a secure case website whereby the clients can log into and run the searches. Once you cross that hurdle, some of the basic fundamentals requirements are:

1. The employer must obtain a written authorization from the potential employee to conduct the background search.
2. A separate authorization will have to be obtain specifically for running a credit history on the candidate.

---

[38] www.NAPBS.com

3. The employer has a duty to provide a written report to the candidate, commonly called and adverse notice, should they chose to not hire the person due to information obtained during the background check.
4. Even though the employer has the requirement to notify the candidate and get their pre-authorization, the PI or screening company is considered a "Consumer Reporting Agency" or "CRA." As such, they must also notify the candidate of any adverse information. An additional letter to the candidate from the CRA must be sent. This opens all kinds of issues with family members getting inquisitive and calling you to try to get more information that they are not entitled.
5. The PI or CRA must do everything in compliance with the Fair Credit Reporting Act (FCRA). The name is miss-leading as it does have restrictions related to credit access but there is much more about the requirements for pre-employment background checks in entirety.
6. The CRA must do everything reasonable to verify information.
7. Should the candidate question the results, the CRA has the responsibility to re-investigate.

Unfortunately there are many companies that do not have full-time Human Resource personnel and they may very likely not be aware of their responsibilities.

When I first started in this business, there were only a couple of databases available and you had to pay a subscriber's fee of $250-500. Now, there are a lot of good databases and seldom do you ever encounter a subscriber's fee. The information broker/databases that I have found to be the best for PI's are as follows:

- TLO (www.TLO.com)
- Clear (www.ClearThompsonReuters)
- IRB (www.IRB.com)

One thing to remember, many law offices and insurance companies have access to some of these same databases. You have to be careful how much you charge the client as they know how much you are paying for the record. Additionally, many of these databases do not allow you to hand over the entire report as generated. You will need to cut and paste into your report form the useful information. If you charge the client $500 for something that cost $15 that may be the last time you see that client. While there is nothing wrong with increasing the cost or including a labor fee in addition to the record cost, you do not need to be perceived as gauging the client. This will provide a better marketing opportunity for getting more cases if you handle the billing justly.

OFF THE WALL MARKETING
Chapter Eight

There are some areas of marketing that is not considered the "norm" in advertising. Some of these work, some don't. For instance, I recently heard a competitor say that one of their marketing tricks was to drop a business card in an elevator and hope that someone would pick it up and need their services. I don't want anyone to pick up my card after 10-15 people have stepped on it. Secondly, what is the chance of getting any real business from this method? Even if you put a card in every elevator in the city, how much business do you really think could be generated from this ploy?. Of course, I have never tried it, so go for it. There are areas of marketing that is considered off the beaten path, but is still good sources for marketing. Some of these include:

- Gyms. There are a lot of business people working out at gyms these days. Most of these gyms have a bulletin board and there are now companies that specialize in putting advertising around the bulletin boards.

- Church Bulletins. With the increase in sexual improprieties surrounding churches, this is a good source. In addition, just because someone goes to church doesn't mean they don't have challenges in their life that they may need an investigator for. Churches are also a good source for pre-employment background searches.

- Shepherd's Guide. This is a publication in many areas that is designed as a yellow page directory for those who profess a belief in God. Others of like faith can find other businesses with like beliefs.

- Telephone Book. Advertising in the telephone book outside of the normal listing can cost thousands of dollars. Most who have ever tried it say it is a waste of money. Secondly, if you call most of those with large advertisements, you will probably find that their telephones are not even being answered. I have actually found them to be very productive. However, as search engines have increased, I have changed the size of my ads. I changed from a full page, to half a page, to a third-page. I have taken that money and invested into internet marketing.

- Internet. This is no longer considered an off-the-wall type of advertising. I can tell you that I have made a tremendous amount of money from being on the Internet. I had my Internet site up on a Wednesday and by Friday, I had three new cases. One turned out to be a long term client who gave me more than $20,000 worth of work in a 4 month period and I just finished a $14,000 case for them. More on this under the Internet chapter.

- Golf. This is the perfect tool for marketing. You get the client away from the telephones and in a better mood because they are doing something besides working. Half the battle in getting a client is to like you as a person. By the end of a round of golf, they will either like you or run from you.

- Tickets. I try to buy tickets to sporting events from time to time and send them to some of my better clients as a thank-you.

- Thanksgiving/Christmas Gifts. During the holidays, I try to get nicely decorated buckets of popcorn, fruit, candy and the like and deliver them to clients. If you can hand deliver them that is the best method. Be sure to put your business cards with the package.

- Calendars. These are a good method of keeping your name in front of the client year round because your name is on them and sitting on their desk. Again with the Internet, fewer people are using printed calendars but if the graphics are well done, you may still find this a good method.

- Pens. Everyone loses pens and likes to get new ones. I deliver these to clients, and eventually they will lose them and hopefully find their way into someone else's hands that might need me!

- Notepads. These are common as a way of marketing. I have found that you have to be careful with a lot of these types of things because if they use them on a daily basis, they get where they don't pay attention to the name and only use them for writing on and overlook the logo

- Baseball hats. I had some hats made with my company name on them and gave them to clients and they all loved them. It is a great way to advertise to others who see the hat as well.

HOW TO RUN A SUCCESSFUL BUSINESS
Chapter Nine

A well-known attorney, F. Lee Bailey once said, "If I were a defendant, I would rather have a good investigator than an attorney." Unfortunately, being a good investigator is just one prerequisite for operating a successful PI business. We have all heard that many doctors are great at being a doctor, but are lousy at being a business owner. The same thing applies to PI's if you do not treat the business like a business. It is important that your frame of mind is right and that you have the mindset of "business" from the very beginning. Overhead is one of the biggest problems facing any business. Therefore, we will discuss some of the things that can make or break a business that include the following:

Office Space:

I am a proponent of PI's having office space versus working from their home. The industry has always had to battle preconceived reputations and having an office outside the house helps project a more professional image. This is a double-edged sword, because I am also the proponent of staying as small as you can for as long as you can. However, in business, there is certain overhead that you simply cannot get around. I have seen PI's hold client meetings in coffee shops, which is definitely a no-no in my book. There is a swing in business to work more out of the house. I mean, if you need office support or a meeting or conference room, you can use places like Office Depot or rent executive offices by the day. I have clients that remember where my office is located and drop by from time to time when they are nearby. It is kind of hard to have clients do this when your office is out of the home. In addition, although other industries are going more to the home-office concept, they typically don't have to battle the poor reputation that our profession is trying to overcome. It may be a good idea to start out at home for the first six months or so, but an office space should be a definite consideration. That doesn't mean you have to go out and rent an entire floor in a high-rise building. You can find some good deals if you take the time to look.

Things to consider when checking into office space include such things as what is the cost per square foot? Who is responsible for the utilities? Who is responsible for air conditioning repairs, plumbing and similar repairs? How much do the "common area" expenses run each year? How easy is the space for you to access? Investigators usually have lap top computers, video cameras, briefcases and other items that they continually carry in and out of the office. I have always sought office space that did not require my staff to carry these things for extended time. Another consideration about whether or not to use an office involves the types of cases you work. Our agency does a lot of surveillance. This means that we have to make duplicate copies of the video and keep them on file in case the client misplaces the video or it gets damaged in the mail. I don't think your home would be an appropriate place for your investigators to hang out and transfer video.

Post Office Box:

Using a post office box makes a lot of sense on one hand, but distracts on the other. If you have a post office box, you never have to change letterhead and other stationary when you move. The use of a post office box can also be seen as a type of security because every lunatic can't find your office. However, in all the years that I have been in business I have never had any problems or threats, much less by someone coming by my office. I initially used a post office box when I started my business. After being in business for a while, I had several corporate executives whom I had developed a good relationship with tell me that they thought I should use a physical address. According to them, a post office box suggested a fly-by-night business that is here today and gone tomorrow. I explained my reasons for using a post office box, but they still believed it to be a matter of perception. I took their suggestion and have received a tremendous amount of comments from clients insuring that I made the right decision.

Telephones:

When a business fails to have a live voice answer the telephones, it should not cease to amaze anyone when the fail. I mean, you spend a lot of time and money trying to bring in the business. Why take a chance on not getting the new case by failing to have your telephone answered? I know many clients that will simply hang up and call someone else if the telephone is not answered by a live person. My system rolls over to call-notes when all of our lines are busy or our office is closed. The call notes, which is part of the services offered by the telephone company, allows me to leave a message in my own voice and the system pages me immediately. I have tried answering services in the past, and that was a mistake. The client is in a hurry and they simply want to give the information to someone right then while they have their file in front of them. The answering service cannot do this so your client will simply call someone else. I have learned that some of this can be side-stepped by giving my clients a stack of our client intake sheets that they can fill out and email or fax to our office. Some clients like this, but others still want to just call the information in. Others clients like being able to e-mail me the information. I make all of these available. I don't care how they give me a new assignment, as long as they give it to me.

We went to a secure internet case management system. This is a huge asset as it saves money on paper and printer cost. The investigators post their notes for the day. A case manager reviews the notes and then approves the notes. The client then receives an email that there is a case update so they can log in and review. They can also initiate a new case from the system. Whatever the method I don't care as long as they get the new case to me!

The next problem with telephones is proper etiquette. Early on in my business, my former partner hired a receptionist while I was out of town. A week later, I was standing by her desk reading a document when the telephone rang. She picked up the telephone and answered it by saying, "tire shop!" I couldn't believe it and asked her if she had ever worked at a tire shop and she replied that she hadn't. She had no idea why she said that, but it was not the way I needed the telephones to be answered. There are a lot of ways to answer a telephone, but one of the more business-like methods is by saying, "Kelmar and Associates, this is __ _____, may I help you?" Putting people on hold is always a treat. You can either have dead silence, a radio while on hold or a message on hold system. Everyone prefers to hear something versus dead silence. The problem with hooking a radio to your telephone system comes when static occurs. You then have to figure out which station would be appropriate for the majority of your clients so as not to give the wrong impression. The message on hold systems are a good alternative, but probably not something that a brand-new business can afford. Later on, however, it should be a definite consideration as you can put messages about your business or the services you offer on tape so that your clients hear this while on hold.

Office Equipment:

Regardless of whether you decide to office in your home or outside of the home, there are certain things that an office has to have to operate correctly. These include a computer, a fax machine, a copy machine, desk, chairs, paper supplies and all of the associated small items. If you are a one-person operation, you may consider a lap top computer rather than a desktop computer. Our job requires us to be out in the field a lot and many reports and record searches can be done remotely using a laptop. As for copy machines, leasing is the way to go. I have purchased 3-4 machines over the years and have finally figured out that leasing is the only way. If you get the right contract, they service the unit, change the toner and update the unit to a newer model in regular intervals. If you own the machine, you have to contend with repairs and having an old, worn out machine. This has changed over the years as well as the "multi-function copy" machines have all of this in one. Be sure to see how many pages can be printed or copied before having to replace toner and print cartridges. The printer may be cheap but the cost to replace these items may quickly exceed the cost of the unit. The cost of repairing these units may reveal that replacing them is cheaper.

As for general office furnishings, I would suggest checking out those stores that handle used office furniture. The prices are much better than new and the furnishings are usually in pretty good shape. Office supply stores like Office Depot also sell furnishings but you will have to put them together.

Investigation Equipment:

A well rounded, all prepared investigator has to have certain items. Others are things that would be nice to have, but aren't absolutely essential. The items that a good investigator will need include the following:

- Tape recorder with the ability to record off telephones.
- Tape measure of at least 100 feet
- Video camera, extra SM cards and batteries.
- 35 mm digital camera.
- Binoculars.
- At least 2 Digital Video Recorders (DVR) and a TV.
- Fake business cards.

Like I said, this is the essential list. There are a lot of other items that could be added, but that varies. The tape recorder is essential for conducting interviews. It also comes in handy when doing surveillance at night when you can jot down notes. A tape measure is essential for working crime scenes, automobile accident scenes and the like. Video cameras and digital cameras are all essential for documentation purposes. The DVR's are required for making back-up copies and extra copies of video for your clients. Fake business cards are important for being able to move about without stirring up too much attention.

General Overhead:

Overhead expenses will make or break a business. Many expenses are taken on when money is coming in and there is no problem paying the bills. However, they are still there when things slow down. Believe me, all businesses regardless of what industry it is, slow down. Knowing this is the key and preparing for it is the answer. Some of the biggest overhead expenses that a PI agency will face include employees, taxes, and travel, telephone and record sources. Controlling these are the keys to success. Then there are all the other items that make up the balance of your budget. Some of these include:

- Bank Charges
- Contract Labor
- Dues and Subscriptions
- Entertainment
- Insurance
- Janitorial Expense
- Licenses & Permits
- Postage
- Professional Fees
- Rental Equipment/Building
- Repair/Maintenance
- Supplies
- Vehicle Expense
- And of course a marketing budget, even if small to begin.

Employees: This is one of the hardest areas to control because you have to pay fairly well if you intend to attract good people. The idea initially is to do as much of the work as possible yourself to save money. This is a good concept, but you have to understand that there comes a point when this is not economically appropriate. If you charge $70-80 an hour for investigations, it doesn't make sense for you to stand and make copies when you can pay someone $10-12 an hour to do that job while you are out making $70-80 an hour. I know one PI that lost clients because he tried to do all things. He tried to answer the phones, type the reports, conduct the record searches and do investigations while finding time to market clients. The reports kept getting to the clients later and later and eventually reports were getting to them 4-6 months after they were ordered. Obviously, that is not the way to do things. I have tried having employees on salary, hourly, part-time, out-sourcing and about every other variation. The idea behind a salary position is that the employee is guaranteed a certain dollar amount. That is good for the company because during busy times, they put in more hours for the same pay. However, during slow times, the company still has to pay them. Paying employees by the hour is OK, except you will catch them spending time on cases at times when they shouldn't, just to keep their hours running.

The problem with any of these is that employees talk among themselves. When this happens, *and it will*, you have the problem of someone feeling like they are not getting paid as much as someone else. I once had a mutiny on my hands and four of my top investigators left to form their own company. Of course if you run the business right, it looks easy and others want to duplicate the success. Then reality sets in. The ex-employees were all out of business in less than 4 months. The whole thing started when one employee started figuring out how many cases the agency averaged per month. He then figured out how much the average case cost and from that, he figured out a general idea of how much the agency was bringing in. He started telling other employees and before you know it, they all had bad attitudes because they didn't feel like they were getting paid enough. Before that had started, everyone was happy with what they were getting paid. Of course, I tried to explain overhead, but they didn't grasp the reality of the situation. I have tried all of the "business experts" philosophies. I have tried making the employees feel like a "team" and giving them more information about the financial situation of the company than they had a right to know. I came to realize what I knew from the beginning. *This is my business. I have all the risk.* I am the one that the bill collectors will come hounding, my name and reputation is at stake and it is my personal livelihood that is at stake. I now only provide employees with a "need to know" amount of information.

I have tried contract labor and out-sourcing, and both have their places. The IRS has gotten critical of those businesses that use contract labor because it was abused for so long. The only time I claim anyone as contract labor is if they have another source of income and they are only working on a job-by-job status and are able to be given a case and work it at their own discretion. Out-sourcing cases is a point of trouble. If you work in this profession very long, you will be faced with having to use a PI in another geographic area to assist in a case. I have written an extremely detailed explanation of what I needed done, the budget, the timetable involved and everything else pertinent. At least 25% of the time, I have trouble with the investigators or their services. I now refuse to out-source a case unless I know the investigator personally. Joining trade associations are a tremendous source for networking. When another PI messes up, it is *your client*, not there's and you are the one that gets caught in the middle.

I always try to keep all cases in house and use my own staff whenever possible. This means that I have a staff of full time employees and those that are part time. Many of the part time employees were full time at one time and they decided to go back to college or their circumstances changed. The problem with part time employees is a lot like out-sourcing. They have other sources of income and your control over them and the product is much less. However, they fill a necessary gap. Full time employees work all week, and they deserve off time. Having part time help is the key to keeping the full time staff from getting burned out.

One of the biggest issues when dealing with employees is different personalities. Each person responds differently and it is your job to figure out how to keep them encouraged and feeling as if they are a vital part of the organization. However, I can assure you that you will be faced with conflicts between employees. It is just part of having any group of people together. Fortunately, in my business, there is less of this because we do so much surveillance and it keeps people in the field where a lot of the office conflicts can't occur. I can tell you from experience that documentation is the key to anything, including employees. It is a common practice to give an employee a verbal warning, followed by a written warning, followed by a suspension or termination if the problem is severe enough. Each one of these situations has to be documented in their personnel file to protect you from a wrongful termination lawsuit. In addition, each employee file should have an application for employment, a PI license application, a photograph, a copy of any tests conducted and a copy of their driver's license. The file should include a copy of their social security card, a completed W-4 employee with holding form and an immigration form documenting that they are a U.S. citizen.

When I took business courses in college, I learned that employee expenses should not exceed more than one-third of your budget. Believe me; if you can keep it to that, you are doing a good job. What that tells you is that if you are charging $80 an hour, you can only expend $30 of this on employees. This means not only their salary, but taxes related to their salary, insurance and the like.

Operating Cost Ratios[39]

Ratios can be used to help measure the effectiveness over cost control. Operating costs can be monitored with the use of direct and indirect operating ratios. Examples of Direct Operating Ratios are:

Direct Labor to Sales = Direct Labor Costs / Sales

Direct Materials to Sales = Direct Materials / Sales

Factory Overhead to Sales = Factory Overhead / Sales

Indirect Operating Ratios can be computed for almost any itemized expense. Two examples are:

Computer Expenses to Sales = Computer Expenses / Sales

Travel Expenses to Sales = Travel Expenses / Sales

Example : Direct Labor Costs are $ 100,000 Factory Overhead is $ 200,000, Computer Expenses are $ 15,000 and Sales were $ 500,000.

Direct Labor to Sales = $ 100,000 / $ 500,000 = .20 or 20%

Factory Overhead to Sales = $ 200,000 / $ 500,000 = .40 or 40%

Computer Expenses to Sales = $ 15,000 / $ 500,000 = .03 or 3%

Operating cost ratios are often used by production managers to monitor trends and identify problems. If a significant change occurs, the problem must be identified as either internal (such as operations) or external (such as economic conditions). Since investors and other outsiders don't have access to operating information, operating ratios are rarely used outside the organization.

---

[39] http://www.exinfm.com/board/operating_cost_ratios.htm

In the PI profession, labor (including sub-contracting) is the highest expense that you will have to deal with as far as expenses. The average rate for pay is $15- $35 per hour. Once you get above this rate you begin to significantly cut into your profit. If you charge $80 per hour and pay an investigator $35, you now have $45 per hour left. All of your other overhead expenses have to come out of this figure. To make it easier let's assume your company conducted a case that generated $3000 in revenue. If you charge $80 per hour, you billed out a maximum of 37.5 hours ($3000 divided by $80).

Revenue $3000
Labor costs   -$1312.50 (37.5 x $35)
                                      $1687.50
Mileage (estimated average) -$ 120.00 (.60 x 200 miles)
                                      $1567.50

You now have to take a percentage out of this for rent, utilities, insurance, payroll taxes, sales tax, clerical, printing expenses, phone expenses, credit card fees, bank fees and the list goes on. You will easily find that you are fighting to make a profit of $500 - $700.

<u>Taxes:</u> This unspeakable *joy* is part of being in business or being an employee. As an employer, you are required to withhold certain taxes from your employee's pay checks that include social security and federal taxes. In some states, you also have state taxes that must be withheld. On the 15th of each month, you have to make a deposit to the taxing agency through your bank to pay the taxes that you withheld. In many states, private investigators have to collect sales tax and pay this on the 20th of each month. When I went into business, my former partner's stepfather was a corporate attorney. He set up the corporation and advised us on how to conduct certain aspects of the business. We charged our clients sales tax only on labor and asked for reimbursement for hotel rooms, video tapes, mileage and the like (including sales tax). My first audit by the state resulted in me having to pay $25,000 because they said I needed to sub-total the invoice and then charge tax. I argued that this was double taxation, which is constitutionally illegal. I went to three tax attorneys who felt confident I could win my case, but it would cost about $100,000 in legal fees to do so. The next time I was audited, everything was OK. I can't tell you the aggravation you feel on the 15th and 20th of the month when you have to take money out of your account to pay these taxes. My recommendation to anyone is to find a good bookkeeper and CPA, as this will pay off in the long run.

Travel Expenses: This is a large expense that includes not only airfare, but mileage reimbursement, hotels and incidentals. Obviously with airfare, the more time that you have to plan a trip, the better deals you can get. Except on long overseas flights, it makes no sense to pay the extra to go first class. The back end of the plane gets there at the same time as the front. It is an expense that can be used better elsewhere. Hotels are relatively the same. You have the business class that range from $70-$150 a night and then the executive class which goes up from $200 per night. When my staff is traveling, they are working and usually don't get back to the hotel until at least 8:00 P.M. It makes no sense to pay $150-250 a night when all you're going to do is lay your head on a pillow. If we were there to enjoy the facility on vacation, it would be different. Otherwise, this money can be used better elsewhere. Mileage reimbursement is a definite consideration. My employees don't get a mileage reimbursement if renting a vehicle while traveling because they are not out anything and the rental car has unlimited mileage. The idea of mileage reimbursement is to compensate someone for the use of their vehicle. Paying a person .54 a mile has been calculated as being appropriate and is designed so that a portion compensates the person for gas and the rest goes for wear and tear on their vehicle. Unfortunately, most people don't put any of this in the bank, and when it is time for repairs or time to replace tires, they may not have the money.

At one time, I gave all my employees a company vehicle and credit cards. I soon found that I was paying for a lot of unnecessary repairs and damage. After I did away with company vehicles, I later had several employees apologize to me for the way they handled the company vehicle. They even admitted that they wouldn't have treated their own vehicle that way. Because of this and the way much of my equipment has been treated, I now have new employees sign an agreement that they will pay for any damages caused by abuse or neglect on their part.

Telephone Expenses: This is an area of expense that can creep up on you quickly. You need at least two telephone lines coming into your office so that if you are on one, your clients can still get through to you on the other. In addition, you need a line dedicated to your computer modem so that you can do record searches and another dedicated to a fax machine. Then, you need cellular telephones. Data, texting plans and similar fees can quickly add up with a group of employees and there must therefore be checks and balances. It is not uncommon for me to have thousands of dollars per month in long distance, cellular and phone line fees. This is the cost of doing business. For many years, I have used two-way radio systems with each investigator being able to talk to others and to the office. This saves cellular time, but I have more cost in equipment and radio airtime.

Factoring: This is a concept by which a company buys your outstanding invoices by paying you 50-80% of what the total bill is worth. They keep the other percentage for loaning you the money up front. This is a good service for those with cash flow crunches, but often prolongs the death of a company. If you are using factoring, it probably means that you are under-capitalized and you have too much overhead or not enough business. You should take a hard look at the business and see where corrections can be made.

For those of you who are just getting started, this next part is for you. If you are in the thinking stages and beginning to put things into action, here is a list of some of the major things you have to do to begin a business:

- Determine if your state has a licensing or regulatory board that over-sees private investigators. There are still 3 states that do not have licensing requirements. However, all others do have a process to go through before becoming a PI. Most will require you to meet certain qualifications as far as experience and education is concerned. You may then have to pass a written test, prove that you have liability insurance and meet more guidelines before you can obtain an agency license. You first have to have an agency license and then an individual PI license.
- Obtain an Assumed Name record by completing a form at the County Clerk's office at the courthouse. This form will demonstrate that you are operating under whatever business name you choose. Although you may or may not incorporate, an assumed name will be required to open a business checking account.
- Contact the State Comptroller or Treasury and obtain an application for sales tax, assuming that your state requires you to collect and pay taxes.
- Contact the IRS and obtain an application for an employer identification number.
- If opening a physical office, you will have to obtain a Certificate of Occupancy from the city/county building inspector's office.
- The Secretary of State's office can be contacted if you are incorporating or creating a company entity.
- Do yourself a favor and hire a CPA. They will take a tremendous load off of your shoulders. They will prepare monthly reports, quarterly and annual reports, IRS returns and keep you compliant in all applicable areas. The cost is usually $150 - $250 per month but is well worth it.

There are other considerations that you should look into while contacting the State Board that regulates private investigators in your state. One of these involves whether or not a PI license allows you to do other services such as process serving. In Texas, you have to have an additional license to do process service. If you want to do executive protection, bounty hunting or something similar, you may have to meet additional requirements.

Billing Procedures:

Billing is one of the more important factors of a company because if you don't bill a client, you won't get paid! The question is, what do you charge per hour and what about other expenses? You have to be realistic when figuring out your hourly rate. All of us would like to be able to charge $300 an hour, but that's not very realistic. You need to determine what is normal for your area. In New York and Los Angeles, you can get more per hour than in other parts of the country. Once again, this is another good reason for going to association meetings. Companies usually lay down their brochures and this often includes their hourly rate. If not, simply call some of the other companies in the area and inquire about their services. A search of Internet sites may also reveal some of this information. You also need to be realistic even after you figure out what the average is. I mean, a lot of these people have been at it for many years and have earned their reputation. You will be starting from scratch. That doesn't mean that you have to be at the bottom, but you need to realize that this is one of the marketing tools you can use. Even though I have been called an expert in various areas of investigations and named one of the top investigators in the entire U.S., I still have competition. At the same time, you don't want to charge too little. I often see this happen where a new company starts up and they charge an unusually low price. Sure, they get a lot of business at the start, but then they are forced to hire more people to keep up with the business. When this happens, you can't do the same work for the same low price. These are the same companies that are here today and gone tomorrow.

After you set your hourly rate, you then need to understand how to bill on the hourly system. Typically, this is done in 15-minute segments. If you did surveillance from 7:00 - 3:10, you should bill for 8.25 hours. Fifteen minutes after the hour is .25 of an hour, 30 minutes after the hour is .5 of an hour, 45 minutes after the house is .75 of an hour. So, if you left your house and proceeded to a surveillance case, you should start charging your hourly rate and mileage from the time you leave your driveway. After you finish your case, you should charge for the return trip to your home or office, whichever is closer. But what if I leave and go to another case? Use your discretion. I usually bill as if I went back to my office and then I bill the next case from my office to the next case. The reason for this is that it is fair for everyone. What if you are working a case and it took you 25 miles to get there and the next case is 45 miles away in a different direction? The first client should not be charged because you have to go in the opposite direction. Likewise, the next client should not be charged more because you went in the opposite direction before you started their case. If you start and finish from the office, it is usually fair. I would suggest that you get a day planner or use mileage log cell phone applications. At the start of each day, before you leave your driveway, write down your beginning mileage. The next morning, do the same thing and you will be able to tell how many miles you went the day before by subtracting the beginning miles the first day from the beginning mileage the second day. Throughout the day, list the case number on the day in the calendar that you worked. This helps you track your cases. There are various cell phone applications that allow you to break this down not only by day but by routes, case/reference numbers and similar categories. Using GPS information also can assist but you need this information not only to bill clients but also for IRS reports.

There are several ways to bill and market. One way is to say that your hourly rate includes everything except mileage or something like hotel and meals. Some clients like this because they don't have all the "incidental" charges. You can offer a client an hourly rate plus expenses or an all-inclusive rate, which is $10-15 higher than the non-inclusive rate. If you charge for your expenses, you should charge anywhere from .50-.70 per mile. Hotel, telephone calls, parking and meals should be just a reimbursed expense. Record searches done in conjunction with surveillance should be the cost of the record plus a 10% profit. Doing only record/database searches requires you to charge more (usually double or triple) for the record. I charge a $25 fee for video because we make a copy and maintain the copy in our office in case the client's copy is lost or destroyed. As for clerical, you may want to charge a standard fee of $30 - $60 per report. If we have to do any transcription, I charge $30 per hour. The trick is to be fair with the client, while being fair to yourself. The outcome of the investigation should have some bearing on the billing. If you knocked a home run on the case, feel free to charge everything. If not much happened, go a little sparingly and make it up on the next case.

Video and Records:

As the owner of the company, you are the "custodian of records" and are responsible for keeping business information intact. I used to keep a hard copy of the file for at least five years (usually more). Since we went to the on-line case management system, we hired a shredding company and got rid of all hard copies. When you obtain video in a case, you need to discuss this with your client. Some clients want the original videotape and others want the PI to keep it. However it is done, you should have a least a copy in your office. Unless I keep the original, all others are put on our server and the DVD or SIM card place in a secured file cabinet.

Product Evaluation:

If you are the owner or supervisor of a company, you have a responsibility to periodically check the level of your services. This includes checking the average time it takes for an investigation to be returned to the client and how you can improve your reports and services. This also means checking up on your employees. If you are busy and have an investigator assigned to a lot of cases, they may feel the pressure. They may try to move from case to case and check on all of them without actually sitting and doing surveillance. The hope is that they will show up just when the person is leaving or mowing their grass. The problem is, this is not the way to do surveillance and your client isn't paying you to check on other cases. Sometimes you will have to take time to run by a location to insure that the investigator is where they are supposed to be and that they are staying the hours they were directed. One way of doing this is by having the investigator shoot some video when they get to a location and every 30 minutes thereafter, regardless of whether anything is happening. Of course, this means that you have to check the video from time to time to keep them honest. It also means that they can simply shoot some video, reset the clock, shoot some more, reset the clock and do it again. However, you have to make an effort to double-check this information periodically. All investigators go through a dry time when nothing seems to be happening. If it lasts too long, that should be an indicator that they are not where they were supposed to be.

Employee Training and Client Contact:

I usually prefer to hire those who have never been involved in the PI profession before. I can train them the way I want them to work and they are also cheaper. However, your entire staff can't be inexperienced. When I hire someone, either I personally train him or her for the first three days or they are put with an investigator with a minimum of 10 years' experience. I help set the mindset and principles that I want instilled in them. I then hand them to one of my senior investigators who keep them for a week. They are then handed off to another senior investigator for another week. Because we do so much surveillance, that is the area that we teach them first. After they pick this up and are able to work cases by themselves, we then teach other specific areas that they need to know. I cross-train everyone to be able to do at least two types of investigations extremely well. I intentionally train only a minimal amount of employees in all facets of investigations. Reality has showed me that employees come and go. There is no need in over-training my competition. When I had the four senior investigators leave my company one time, I realized how much this paid off. Although I didn't want to stand in the way of their success, I also didn't want to help them take my clients from me. It became apparent that they couldn't because they didn't know how to run license plates, where to get certain records and similar pertinent information. I later discovered that they had taken a lot of my internal forms and logs. Anyone that works for you can take this information and use it and if you are in business long enough, this will probably happen.

I have case managers that know some of my sources and many of my internal safeguards. Outside of them, no one in my organization is capable of running the entire organization. This is self-preservation. I also learned through experience that the more one of my investigators talk to my clients, the less my client needs me. If allowed, a bond could grow and I could lose many of my clients. Therefore, my case managers or I are the only ones in my organization that are allowed to have direct communication with the client unless I specifically request them to contact the client. Some say this is over-protection (and it may be) but I have seen others lose their whole livelihood by not taking precautions. We would all like to think that our employees are ours from now on and that loyalty will never be an issue. Realistically, we know this is just not the way things work.

To take this a step further, I require all employees to sign confidentiality and no-compete agreements. The document means that all clients, reports, videos, logs and other internal information is strictly for the use and benefit of Kelmar and Associates and cannot legally be used outside the agency. It also means that they agree that they cannot engage in the PI profession within a 100-mile radius of Kelmar and Associates for a one-year period after leaving the company. Attorneys will argue about the validity of these contracts, but it serves as a deterrent and is better than not having one.

USING AN OPERATIONS MANUAL

Each employee that walks through the door should be given an operations manual to assist them in doing their job better. During training, a lot of information is thrown at them. When they are on their own, they need something to refer to that will help answer questions and keep them on track. In addition, it is important for them to see professionalism and this is another way of demonstrating this to them. An example of an operations manual is as follows:

OPERATIONS MANUAL

MISSION STATEMENT:

The mission of Kelmar and Associates is to provide professional investigative services to accomplish the goals of our clientele utilizing the most effective and state-of-the-art methods available. Kelmar will augment our client's abilities to enable them to make informed, problems solving decisions in their ever-changing business environment.

GOALS AND OBJECTIVES:

The goals of Kelmar and Associates are to maintain a definite presence in the markets currently being serviced and to expand to other markets while maintaining a consistent work product. The objectives are to increase the profit/loss ratio while becoming more lean and competitive.

OFFICE PROCEDURES

*Some of this has changed for my company based on our going to a secure case management site.

CASE ASSIGNMENTS:

The client typically calls the investigation assignments into the office. They may however, be assigned via the facsimile machine, regular mail or e-mail. In either case, the appropriate information must be obtained from the onset to insure maximum effectiveness. The information should be documented on the *Client Data Sheet* to conform to uniformity and consistency. The information that should be obtained includes the following:

The client's business name, their address and telephone number, along with the contact person who the report should be sent to.

The client's file number and the date that the incident in question occurred.

The objectives of the investigation (EX: surveillance, background check...)

The name, address, telephone number, date of birth, social security number, driver's license number, physical description, vehicles known to drive and other similar information should be obtained concerning the subject being investigated. If insurance related, the subject's doctor and next appointment should be obtained.

The office personnel should determine if there are time restraints, deadlines or other time factors.

An agreement concerning the cost of the investigation should be reached before the investigation is initiated.

The case should then be entered into the *Case Log Book* and assigned a case number.

A file folder should then be set up for the case, which should include a copy of the city map book for the street (if surveillance), a blank *case log/time sheet* and any other pertinent records. The file should then be assigned to an investigator.

TELEPHONE MESSAGES:

Office personnel are to receive messages, transfer to the appropriate extension or otherwise notify the recipient of the message. All messages should be returned within an hour if in the office or a twenty-four hour period if in the field, excluding weekends and holidays.

RECORD CHECKS:

The investigations that require record checks should be conducted in one of three ways:

The local office should have a computer system that allows them to access the local courthouse records. Office personnel should conduct these searches unless the office has expanded enough to support an "inside investigator".

A search or review of local records that are not on the computer or which require a physical review should be assigned to an outside field investigator for completion.

All other record searches should be conducted by utilizing the services available through the home office of Kelmar & Assoc.

At no time is the use of outside vendors or agencies allowed without prior written consent from the home office. The company maintains accounts and resources for a wide variety of record and database access.

SURVEILLANCE

SURVEILLANCE EQUIPMENT:

Before surveillance is conducted, the proper equipment should be obtained to fulfill the goals in a professional manner. The following are some of the items necessary:

A. *Video Camera:* A standard off-of-the-shelf video camera can be utilized and has many benefits over the larger, more expensive commercial units. The size and weight allows the investigator to hold the camera for extended periods and it can be versatile to be used in different cases for concealment.

B. *Digital Camera:* This is no longer an absolute essential tool of an investigator because the video can tell so much more than a still photo. However, a digital camera may still be necessary if an accident scene or other evidence documentation is needs completed that is more appropriately conducted via this equipment.

C. *DVR and TV:* These are essential office items that are needed to review the video obtained and to make a master copy as well as extra copies.

D. *Camera Lenses:* It is important that a good long-range lens be obtained that has the zoom-in/zoom-out ability. This will allow the investigator to remain at a greater distance from the subject and still obtain good quality video. A good long-range lens should be capable of at least 300 feet, and preferably 600-1000 feet. In addition, a second smaller lens should be obtained for situations when the long-range lens is too much and the camera lens is not enough. A "doubler" is adequate and doubles the ability of the camera's own lens.

E. *Surveillance Vehicle:* Not every vehicle is appropriate for surveillance use. A vehicle should not be anything that would attract attention, but instead, be common enough to fit in and be over-looked. Although vans offer the most comfort for the investigator, they are more difficult to hide behind other vehicles for concealment, require more attention when operating, and require more space for parking and other factors which prohibit them from being good surveillance vehicles. In addition, most people who think of PI's assume that they use vans, drawing further suspicions to a possibly already suspicious person. The vehicle selected should be organized so that the investigator can quickly reach the video camera and other equipment.

F. *Window Tinting:* The vehicle(s) that will be used for surveillance should have the maximum window tint allowed by State Law for concealment and coolness during hot summer days.

G. *Plexiglas:* The investigator should invest in two pieces of Plexiglas that are cut to duplicate the driver and passenger door windows. The Plexiglas should then have dark, reflective window tint applied to them. When sitting still conducting surveillance, the Plexiglas pieces should be placed in back of the windows to further darken the interior for concealment. Note: It is against traffic laws to drive with the Plexiglas pieces in place.

H. *Curtains:* The investigator should obtain some lightweight cloth (preferably in the same color as the vehicle's interior) use as curtains. The material should be hung behind the front seats to block sunlight and provide additional concealment.

I. *Window Shades:* The investigator should invest in several different front windshield shades. Again, they should be as plain as possible to not draw attention to the vehicle. The shades can be used while parked in conjunction with the Plexiglas and curtains to provide maximum concealment.

J. *Gym Bag:* A good gym bag should be obtained and kept with the investigator at all times in case the subject enters a building and may be involved in some type of work or physically strenuous activity that requires video documentation. The bag should have a sturdy bottom to secure and protect the camera. Numerous "pin" holes should be poked or drilled into the bag to form a circle for the lens to see through. An entire circular hole is not necessary because one advantage of a video camera is that it does not require a totally unobstructed view.

K. *Camera Briefcase*: Often, a subject may enter a building where video needs to be obtained discretely and a gym bag is not suitable. An old briefcase that still looks decent on the exterior should be obtained. It will have to be wide enough to set a video camera in and shut the lid on. A black case is preferred. Once a suitable briefcase is found, place the camera in the bottom, mark and drill a hole in the bottom and obtain a suitable bolt for securing the camera. Next, mark the circle where the lens will be and use the smallest drill bit available to drill small holes inside the circle. Again, the entire circle does not have to be removed as a sufficient amount of holes will accomplish the same task. If the case is black, after drilling the holes, use black shoe polish or leather dye to daub into the holes to make them inconspicuous. When used, the camera will have to be positioned, turned on and adjusted and then left on the entire time. The use of an extended battery pack may be necessary. Brief cases for surveillance can be ordered however, they begin at approximately $1,500 and go up.

L. *Extended Play Battery Pack*:   For approximately $60 an extended battery pack should be obtained for supplying power to the video camera when away from the vehicle. The batteries will supply power up to 6.5 hours.

M.   *DC Power Cord*:   A cigarette lighter cord can be obtained for approximately $25 which will allow the video camera to be operated off of the vehicle's car battery.

N. *Extra SIM Cards:* An investigator should always have additional SIM cards to store the video on while shooting long periods of activity. Most video cameras have hard drive storage but now many have either/or and memory capabilities need to be addressed before required.

O. *Pen-light flashlight:* A small flashlight or pen-light should be kept in the surveillance vehicle for use in the dark for making adjustments to the camera, writing notes, etc… without drawing attention by turning on the interior lights.

P. *Pocket tape recorder:* A digital micro pocket size audio recorder should be obtained for dictating notes, recording conversations, etc…

Q. *Covert Cameras*: You need to continue to evaluate your inventory of covert cameras as well as review current trends in technology. In doing so, you can have the best equipment available when needed.

Other equipment can come in handy and will make the job easier. However, the items listed above are essential equipment for any investigator.

PRELIMINARY CHECK:

Before the actual surveillance is initiated, certain preliminary checks should be conducted which include the following:

Address Verification: An attempt should be made to verify the address provided for the subject. This should be done through database searches, a social security trace, appraisal district and/or property tax records. While checking the records, attention should be given to others on the same street with the same last name that may be related to the subject.

Map verification: A check of the address should be conducted using an internet site like Yahoo or Google maps to double-check the spelling, correct direction (Ex: East or West Main), to identify the block and the quickest route to the address.

Zip Code Verification: The map should be checked against the zip code to insure that it matches the reported zip code. In addition, double-check the street to make sure that it is in the suburb and that there are not more streets elsewhere with the same name.

Google Earth: A review of the property and general area on Google Earth can provide a visual of the address. This will give you a pre-determined idea of possible surveillance locations, if the house is a one or two story house and other useful information.

Assumed Names: Depending on the type of case, it may warrant conducting several record checks prior to conducting surveillance. For example: If you are conducting a worker's compensation investigation, check the county assumed name records to determine if the subject has a business in their name. Likewise a check of the Secretary of State's records may assist in this same goal

Preliminary Surveillance: The initial surveillance should be conducted during daylight hours to properly identify the house number, descriptions of the house, vehicles and general area. The initial notes should include:

> House description: A description of the house should be noted and should include a statement similar to the following, "The claimant's house was situated on the northwest corner of Hill and Main St. and it is described as a one-story white wood frame structure with a two car garage and a chain link fence around the backyard". During the different seasons, written (or at least mental) notes should be taken regarding the length of the grass (need cutting soon?), Christmas decorations (are there indications that the claimant may be getting ready to decorate), or similar activities.

> Vehicle descriptions: A description of each vehicle should be noted and should include a statement similar to the following; "Upon arrival, there was a red 2013 Ford Expedition parked in the driveway with license plate number LTD-121, which is registered to.....".

> Surveillance Positioning: A suitable surveillance location should be identified that will provide the best *discrete* observation of the subject's house.

The investigator should attempt to park on a side street, on the next street over to look between houses at the subject's house, in a business parking lot or other similar areas. The investigator should attempt to park near other vehicles so that should the subject leave and pass the investigator's vehicle, it will be just one of several vehicles and will not draw special attention. In addition, the investigator should attempt to park in the shade to be more comfortable and to make it darker inside the vehicle to prohibit anyone easily seeing that someone is sitting in the vehicle.

The investigator should park facing the same direction as other vehicles nearby to prevent drawing attention. It may be necessary to park with the back of the investigator's vehicle facing the subject's house and to conduct surveillance using the rear and side mirrors. If the investigator is forced to identify themselves to suspicious neighbors, they will assume that the person being watched is in front of the investigator's vehicle even though the person is actually at the opposite end of the street. This will help prevent the neighbors from tipping off the subject and will assist in discreteness.

At no time should an investigator park closer than 10-12 houses from the house of the subject being investigated to prevent suspicions on the part of the claimant. If the subject engages in physical activity, the investigator should be able to move closer while the subject's back is turned or attention is diverted. In addition, if a neighbor calls the police regarding a suspicious person sitting in the neighborhood and the police arrive, the subject may not see the police make contact with the investigator and will therefore draw less attention towards the investigator. Depending on the neighborhood, it may be advisable to identify yourself to the owners of the house that you have decided to sit while conducting surveillance. This will put the owners at ease and prevent them from calling the police and drawing attention to the investigator. **The client and the subject being investigated should never be disclosed.**

SURVEILLANCE:

The investigator should always remember the purpose of surveillance; to observe, document and video tape any and all activities. This is to be done with absolute discreteness, without interfering or altering the subject's activities. The investigator should never engage in the following:

A. *Violate Laws*: At no time should the investigator violate the local, state or federal laws. In addition, no rule or regulation of the State Board of Private Investigations is to be breached.

B. *Traffic Violations:* The investigator is legally bound to adhere to the existing traffic laws, speed limits and other traffic controls.

C. *Entrapment*: At no time should the investigator plant evidence, create obstructions or initiate circumstances that would alter the subject's regular activities.

D. *Trespassing:* The investigator should not enter onto the subject's premises, yard, house, vehicles or other property of the subject.

E. *Disclosures:* The client confidentiality rules are to be strictly adhered to. A private investigator, by law, is not required to identify their client or the person they are investigating to anyone (including the police). An investigator is required to identify to police that they are a P.I. and to show the appropriate identification but not disclose confidential information.

Length of Surveillances:

The length of each surveillance period is contingent upon the number of hours requested and/or the monetary cap agreed upon with the client. However, since the client is paying for mileage every time the investigator goes to the subject's house, the number of trips should be minimized. Surveillance should encompass at least 1.5 hours unless the subject is obviously not home.

The initial surveillance period should be conducted in the daylight to allow for proper identification of house numbers, vehicles, etc…

Surveillance should be conducted in the early morning hours, mid-afternoon, and late afternoon/early evening hours in an attempt to identify when the subject is most likely to be active. Additional surveillance should then be centered around the times that the most activity is believed to occur.

Vehicle Surveillance Techniques:

Surveillance is an art that will become easier the more it is done, as well as when better equipment is utilized. The key to surveillance is getting as close to the subject as possible, without getting too close to arouse suspicions. To do this and to maintain the proper distances requires constant thought and observation. Unlike the movies, a real investigator cannot park directly in front of the subject's house or follow directly behind the subject's car. Each surveillance is different from the others performed and the investigator will have to constantly adapt to the situations and geographic area that they become involved. Some of the basic techniques are:

A. *Positioning of Vehicle*: As previously stated, positioning of the investigator's vehicle in relation to the subject's house or vehicle is extremely important as it will have a direct bearing on how much suspicion is created. At no time should the investigator position themselves closer than half a block from the subject's house. The investigator can always move closer if absolutely necessary, but being too close initially will draw immediate attention to the investigator. Positioning the vehicle with the back facing the subject's house will help alleviate any suspicions on the part of inquisitive neighbors.

Whenever possible, the investigator should attempt to park on a side street or on the next street over. If the subject's house (and cars) can be seen from the next street over by looking between houses, this will provide great concealment. If the subject leaves in their vehicle, the investigator should have ample time to travel parallel to the subject and fall behind them at the next intersection. If a foreclosed house or repossessed house is identified on the street and is still the appropriate distance from the subject's house, the investigator may be able to sit in the driveway of the vacant house.

B. *Following the subject:* Once the subject leaves in their vehicle, the investigator should have already checked the neighborhood out to see which streets will get people living on that street to the main streets, shopping areas, schools, etc... the fastest. Most people are subjects of habit and will usually take the same routes. If the investigator has determined that there are no nearby streets for the subject to turn on, greater distance can be allowed before pursuit is initiated. However, if this is not the case, immediate pursuit will be necessary and additional distance can be allowed once the subject gets out to a main street where the investigator can blend in better.

When following a subject on residential streets, the investigator should attempt to time it so that just as the subject makes a turn, the back of the car will be seen while the subject will be concerned with making the turn and not with the traffic behind them. The investigator may have to stop by other vehicles on the side of the road temporarily to re-establish the proper distance between the cars or to prevent the investigator from coming up directly behind the subject at a red light. Care will have to be taken that once the light turns green, the investigator has sufficient time to get through the light as well.

Once the vehicle reaches a two-lane roadway, expressway or other street with more vehicle traffic, the pursuit becomes easier and but can eventually be harder. Following the subject becomes easier because there are more vehicles to conceal the investigator's vehicle. However, these additional vehicles can cause congestion and delays that will allow the subject to be lost. When the subject reaches a road with two or more lanes of traffic, the investigator should attempt to stay out of the same lane of traffic to prevent the subject from constantly seeing the same vehicle behind them. The amount of traffic, the number of traffic lights and other traffic factors will determine how much distance you can give the subject. Ideally, the investigator should be at least one lane over from the subject and at least 4-5 cars back. When following on an expressway, the investigator should always attempt to stay one lane closer to the exits than the subject is. That way, if the subject recklessly crosses two or more lanes of traffic to reach an exit, the investigator will not attract the same attention as they are already in the nearest lane to the exit. Also if there is an exit that allows traffic to exit the highway, continue on the access road without stopping and provides another entrance ramp to the highway, the investigator can exit the highway, travel down the access road and immediately re-enter the highway.

When following a vehicle, the investigator should use the terrain and other vehicles to their advantage. Hiding behind a truck or van allows the investigator's vehicle to be out of view of the subject even though the investigator can see through the van's windows and watch the roof of the subject's car. Hiding behind larger vehicles even while moving is a great technique. To keep an eye on the subject's car, occasionally move your vehicle to the far left or right in the lane to see around the vehicle in front of the investigator. When the subject is in a lane that has to turn right, the investigator can turn into the business on the corner (such as a gas station & pull up next to the pump), wait for the subject to turn and then continue behind them. When the subject is on a main street with a lane that turns onto the highway's access road, the investigator (if the first car in the right lane) can proceed straight and stop at the red light while the subject merges onto the access road. The investigator can then make a right on red and continue on the access road. If the subject turns onto a different street, the investigator may be able to turn one street before the street or one street after the one the subject turned on and the subject can then be paralleled. The key is to watch for the subject's vehicle between house and attempt to come up to the intersections just as the subject is passing through or turning.

There may be times when the subject is especially attentive to those around them and after having followed them for quite a while, it would be in the best interest of all involved to drop the surveillance to discourage any suspicions. There is always another day, unless you blow it and make the subject aware that they are being investigated.

C. Pedestrian Surveillance: Following a subject who is walking or riding a bicycle presents special problems because the investigator will probably have to leave the security and effectiveness of their vehicle at some time during the surveillance to follow the subject. If the subject parks in a downtown area, the investigator may be forced to park and follow on foot due to the numerous one-way streets commonly found in downtown areas. Even if the subject is walking a long distance on the same street, chances are there will not be a place for the investigator to pull over every time they need to move up to catch up to the subject. In addition, the subject may abruptly enter a building with many offices and having to find a parking space and catch up to the subject will more than likely result in the subject being lost. For these reasons, the investigator should attempt to park whenever the subject does (or whenever he gets off a bus, etc…). The investigator should attempt to walk on the opposite side of the street and behind the subject. While doing so, the investigator has to pay attention to traffic movements, cross-walks, windows that reflect images which will provide the subject with the opportunity to see behind them and openings, stores and other cover for concealment in case the subject stops. If for some reason, the subject stops and begins to look around, turns around and walks back in the opposite direction or some other spur of the moment activity, the investigator should not be startled and should maintain the direction without altering. This way, the investigator will not draw attention and will continue to look like any other person who has his or her own destination to reach.

If the subject enters a building, the investigator will have to hustle to the building to see where the subject goes. This may mean that you will have to enter the same elevator. If this occurs, you should wait for the subject to punch the floor button first. The investigator can then punch the button for the floor above where the subject is exiting and then walk back down the stairway in an attempt to catch up. In any event, you will then know what floor the subject is on and a check with the offices on the floor using a suitable pre-text can determine which office they entered. The investigator may wish to get off of the elevator on the same floor, exit and walk in the opposite direction of the subject and appear uncertain of which office you need while watching the subject.

Following a subject who enters a mall, stadium or other large public facility usually does not pose many problems. It is a common fact that the majority of people do not look up when walking. Therefore, you should put your video camera in a bag or briefcase and proceed to follow the subject. If they are on the first level at a mall, the investigator should position themselves on the floor above, keeping behind the subject while peering down at them. Video inside the mall will surprisingly not draw too much attention, even if the camera is in plain view. If the subject ends up on the same level as the investigator, concealment can be obtained by entering shops and watching the subject through the glass storefront windows while appearing to browse at merchandise.

Following a subject into a restaurant may or may not be a good idea, depending on the nature of the investigation. If the investigator has not been seen by the subject before, and there is reason to believe that vital information may be learned if the subject's conversations are heard, the investigator may want to enter the restaurant and request a table near the subject. The investigator should order immediately, order something quick to prepare and should attempt to exit the restaurant just ahead of the subject.

One of the problems with following the subject out in the open and on foot is that it allows the person to observe the investigator. If the same face keeps popping up wherever the subject goes, they may get suspicious. Therefore, if more than one investigator is available, it may be wise to switch off.

D. Public Transit Surveillance: If a subject takes a bus or similar public transportation, the way the investigator handles this is dependent upon the number of investigators available. The best case scenario would be to have at least two investigators with one following the bus and the other riding the bus with the subject. However, if only one investigator is available, they should strive to keep the bus in sight so those people getting on and off at each bus stop can be observed. In downtown areas, this can be difficult due to the frequent stops that the bus makes. The investigator may have to pass the bus occasionally and then pull over to wait on it. Once again, the investigator should pay attention to possible parking spots as they are traveling so that the subject can be followed on foot when they exit the bus.

E. Other Areas of Surveillance: Additional techniques will have to be utilized and altered as individual situations arise. However, some of the more common places that you may follow subjects to include parks, gyms, bars, doctor's offices, courthouses and similar places. The goals of the investigation should be considered before creating unnecessary suspicions by getting too close to the subject in one of these areas. For example, if you are conducting a worker's compensation investigation, there is probably no need to follow the subject into a doctor's office. An exception to this would be if you are having a difficult time locating the subject but learn of a doctor's appointment. You may have to enter the office to identify the subject. If the person goes into a bar or gym, it may or may not be important to obtain video inside. If you need to document their physical abilities, employment activities or similar information then video may be necessary. If this is the case, you may have to rely on the briefcase or bag. If it is a bar, they may not allow these items inside. The investigator can then try to walk in with the camera by telling them that a friend is having a party and they wanted to have it filmed. Or, the investigator may be able to have a female (if the investigator is not a female) accompany them with a large purse in which to hide the camera. Other possible scenarios may be available as well, depending on the individual situation.

CONTACT WITH POLICE DURING SURVEILLANCE:

It is not uncommon for neighbors to call the police regarding the investigator being a "suspicious person". Again, this should not pose a problem if the investigator is properly positioned far enough from the subject's house. If the investigator sees the police approaching, they should attempt to hold their badge and ID up as the officer approaches so that the officer will be more receptive. It is not uncommon for an officer to continue on without stopping if they see the identification. However, if they stop, the investigator should be extremely polite and cooperative. The investigator, by law, has to identify themselves and their reason for being there. The investigator does not have to identify the person being investigated or the client as this falls within the client confidentiality laws. Always attempt to check the officer's name badge while talking as the officer was found to be related to the subject being investigated in at least one case worked by Kelmar.

POSSESSION OF A FIREARM:

Kelmar and Associates does not commonly work cases that require a firearm be carried for personal protection. The current law in the State should be reviewed regarding carrying a firearm by an private investigator. In the State of Texas, the law prohibits this unless they are also a certified police officer. Regardless of the law, it is the policy of Kelmar to not carry a firearm while conducting investigations. This includes the person, vehicles, briefcase or other property utilized during the performance of the investigation. If a case warrants an investigator carrying a firearm, prior written consent has to be obtained from the home office. Failure to abide by this rule is immediate grounds for termination and termination of any licensing agreements.

NOTE TAKING/REPORT WRITING

NOTE TAKING:

Taking clear, detailed notes during any investigation is extremely important during any investigation but is more difficult in surveillance cases. Proper notes should be taken during the investigation and the file updated after each time the case is worked. If the investigator gets sick, leaves the company or other situations arise, the follow-up investigator will have very little to work with if the file notes are not current. The details also seem to be forgotten after other cases are worked and time goes by, therefore the notes should be written while they are still fresh in the investigator's mind.

If the office has more than one investigator, the lead investigator/manager should review the other investigator's files periodically to ensure that notes are current and that there is not some type of records or other activity that has been over-looked. A recommended review of the files should be done at least once a week by the supervisor.

The notes should always be written in the *third person* to present a more unbiased and professional revelation of the facts. It is recommended that the notes use the phrase, "Kelmar personnel" and should be interchanged with "The investigator". For example, a sentence may read, Kelmar personnel returned to the claimant's house at approximately 1:00 P.M. on December 3, 1994.

It is also recommended that the term "approximately" be utilized when relating a specific time. This may prevent unnecessary scrutiny of you or the report by an aggressive attorney.

Surveillance Notes:

Each investigator has their own method of taking notes during surveillance which they feel comfortable with and which works for them. Whichever method the person chooses, it should be a process that is effective and consistent. The investigator may want to have a small notepad on a base that is attached to the windshield or dash through suction cups. The investigator may wish to have a briefcase in the seat beside them to use as a desktop for scribbling notes on a pad. Some investigators prefer to use a tape recorder and transfer the notes to paper later. If the tape recorder method is chosen, the investigator will have to be constantly aware of their location in respect to the person being followed so that they do not raise the recorder to speak into it when they are directly behind the subject in traffic or in other situations where this may be seen. In addition, the investigator should always have a small pocket size notebook available to take notes on when the person is being followed on foot, in a building or other similar situations.

After the manner in which notes are to be taken is satisfied, the next step is the proper taking of notes. Commonly this involves the who, what, when, where and why scenario and includes the following:

A. Initial Notes: The investigator should indicate when the surveillance was initiated which will include the date and time, as well as the address or location. A description of the house should be noted along with any unusual or distinctive items observed. The area of town should be indicated which should indicate the closest main streets that the reader may recognize. The initial notes should list a description of the vehicles, boats, trailers or other similar vehicles. The type, year, color, license plate number and registration information should be listed. A typical starting paragraph may be related as follows:

Kelmar personnel initiated surveillance at the claimant's reported address of 130 Roberts St. at approximately 1:00 P.M. on November 11, 1994. The house is located in the Oakwood Subdivision in Southeast San Antonio near Military Dr. and Lackland Air Force Base. The residence is described as a one-story white wood- frame structure with a two-car garage, a chain link fence around the backyard and a decorative water fountain in the front yard. Upon arrival, a red 1991 Chevy Camaro, license number 124-CBN, which is registered to Daniel Ybarra, 130 Roberts St., San Antonio, was parked in the driveway.

B. Body of Notes:

Once the preliminary facts are stated, entries should then be made based on the observations. If the subject leaves in a vehicle, the investigator should attempt to indicate which streets the subject traveled on, which businesses they stopped at, any activities that they were involved in, as well as other similar information. For example:

At approximately 1:10 P.M., the subject entered the red Chevy Camaro (license 123-BYU) and turned right on Lewis St., left on Roberts Lane, headed north on IH-35, exited on Malone and stopped at the Exxon convenience store at the corner of Malone and Division. The subject then began to pump gasoline into the tank of the car (see video) and paid the attendant before returning to the car.

The body of the notes should be specific in regards to the activities and their relation to the injury. If the subject is supposed to have an injury right wrist and shoulder, you should indicate that the subject picked up the newspaper, opened the door or performed other activities with the injured hand. If the subject has an injured back and is observed outside with only a T-shirt on without a back brace on, indicate the same in the report. If you had the opportunity to observe the claimant at a doctor's appointment with a cane or back brace and subsequent surveillance resulted in the cane or back brace not being observed, indicate the same in the report. In short, any activities that occur by the subject or at the subject's house should be indicated in the report. The report should only indicate what was determined or what activities were observed, without any bias or opinions being indicated.

C. Report Conclusion:

Most reports do not require a paragraph at the end entitled, "conclusion". However, the investigator may want to indicate certain information or make suggestions that would be appropriate at this time. For example:

Surveillance was conducted at the subject's residence on eight different days. On six of these dates, the subject was observed outside of their residence working in the yard, talking to neighbors and walking the neighborhood for exercise. The client may wish to consider additional surveillance due to the subject's active lifestyle to better document the subject's activities and abilities.

Most of the time, any information important enough to put into a conclusion should also be indicated in the summary paragraphs. The wording should be changed to not sound as repetitive and to further place the ideas in the reader's mind.

D. *Proof-Reading the Report:*

It is the investigator's responsibility to provide the report information to the clerical staff in a manner that will allow them to easily type the notes. If the notes are hand written, they should be as much like the final copy as possible to prevent both the investigator and the secretary from having to make too many corrections and alterations. Likewise, if notes are dictated on tape or provided in some other manner, they should be easily typed. It is the investigator's job to relate the notes in a clear, concise and logical order. The only items the secretary should be asked to enter that are not in the actual notes are information regarding the license plate registrations or other records. However, blanks should be left in the notes to indicate to the secretary that the record needs to be placed there. Often, the investigator should go ahead and write record information into the notes to keep the logical sequence of facts flowing properly in the report.

Once the notes are turned into the secretary, the report should be typed, printed out on rough draft paper and returned to the investigator to proofread for facts and corrections. Once the investigator makes the corrections, the secretary should make the noted corrections and then proceed with printing the final report.

E. Report Attachments:

The clerical staff should print the final copy of the report out, including a cover sheet and attach certain records with the report. The records should include copies of license registrations, social security trace reports, record checks conducted and any other useful information obtained during the investigation.

WRITTEN REPORTS:

The secretary is responsible for typing the written field notes, tape recorded notes or other records into the standard report format of Kelmar and Associates.

The rough draft is to be printed and proofread by the investigator involved and returned to the secretary for corrections and completion of the final report. The report format is to include the following:

The *Cover Sheet* is printed on letterhead and will include the client's name, the contact person's name, the client's file number, the name of the person being investigated, the date of the incident in question, the Kelmar case number and a statement of disclaimer.

The *Request of Client* will be the first paragraph on the second page and indicates whom the client and the contact person is. In addition, the purpose and goals of the investigation will be re-stated along with the name of the person(s) being investigated. The name of the investigator(s) assigned will also be identified.

The *Summary* paragraph(s) will be the second sub-heading on the second page and will summarize the findings and major topics of the investigation. NO OPINIONS are to be included anywhere within the report as we are to provide only factual events and documentation. The investigator may include a statement indicating that additional surveillance or investigation time may be needed to further document the client's goals.

The *Details of Investigation* is the third paragraph that is the body of the report and provides the details and findings of the investigation. Any information obtained through record searches, surveillance or other sources should be included in this section.

The *Conclusion* may or not be necessary. Typically, this is used to support the need for additional investigative work, suggest alternatives or relate similar information.

BACKGROUND INVESTIGATIONS

Background investigations are conducted for various reasons and may be done in conjunction with surveillance cases. The client may wish to obtain a general idea of the person's character, or they may want to determine specific information such as criminal history, civil history, employment history, hidden assets and other information. Regardless of the goals of the investigation, the same general records and procedures will be used during the investigation.

All records obtained should meet certain criteria. Because of the nature of the PI business, all records and reports are subject to scrutiny and may end up in a court. We owe our clients responsible record searches that will not create difficulties for the client or for Kelmar. Therefore, all records obtained *shall be legal* to have, possessed and to use. If a record and the source of the record cannot be used and identified, do not waste our time and the client's money to obtain them.

The majority of record searches conducted will be done through public records at the county level, with some being obtained from the State and Federal levels. These records can be obtained through local computer links, on-sight research, through the mail and by telephone calls. Seldom will you (the field investigator) have to use outside data sources. These in fact, are discouraged because of the liability and costs. Unfortunately, a large majority of the database services available offer records that are not legal to possess. Because of this, record searches through outside agencies present one of the greatest areas for possible liability and negligent lawsuits against the investigator. Kelmar therefore restricts the use of outside sources without prior written authorization.

PUBLIC RECORDS:

For a more detailed outline of the types and uses of public records, obtain a copy of "Private Investigating-Made Easy", by Kelly E. Riddle (available through most bookstores or through Kelmar).

Public records are those records, which by law, are accessible to the general public. However, most people do not know what records are out there or how to obtain them. Each local office should have a computer link to the county courthouse records so that a search can be conducted without leaving the office. If a record is found, the investigator can then go to the courthouse and review the actual file.

County Records:

The local county courthouse is a source where the majority of the record searches will be conducted. The records are housed primarily in the county clerk's office and the district clerk's office. The records found in each office are as follows:

County Clerk's Office

1. Assumed Names
2. Marriage Records
3. Livestock Brands
4. Property Deed Records
5. Financial Statements (Debts)
6. Birth records
10. Tax liens
8. Inheritance records
10. Mechanic's Liens
10. Criminal records

District Clerk's Office

1. Civil Records
    a. divorce cases
    b. personal injury cases
    c. child support cases
    d. property seizures
    e. general damage cases

2. Criminal Records

In addition to these records, there are the County Tax Assessor's records and the County Appraisal District records. Both deal with the ownership of property, however, only one will normally list the mortgage company for the property.

State Records:

There are several offices at the State level that are open to the general public and should be utilized by an investigator. These include:

State Comptroller's Office---will provide the owners of businesses, and will indicate who is paying taxes on oil leases, hotels, mineral rights, interstate trucking and more.

Secretary of State's Office---will provide information on companies that are incorporated.

State Parks and Wildlife---will conduct a review of their records for any vessels (boats) listed to a person.

State Dept. of Public Safety---will conduct driver's license history searches.

State Boards---will provide information on professional licenses (doctors, lawyers, PI's, etc...).

Federal Records:

Bankruptcy records---will provide tremendous amount of information if the subject has a bankruptcy on file.

Civil records---involves disputes between the government and individuals.

Criminal records

Municipal Records:

Police Department surveys---some departments will provide a survey of their records and provide all of the calls associated with a person and/or address.

Municipal Court records---a check of these records will provide information on municipal traffic tickets and the ticket can be reviewed.

Utility records---a written request can be faxed/mailed to the local utility company to obtain the current record for the subject.

Other records/Outside Agency Databases:

As previously stated, no outside agencies/databases can be utilized without the prior written permission of Kelmar. This is for the protection of all parties involved and is strictly enforced.

Kelmar maintains several databases that can be used by other offices and include:

Social Security Trace---with a known social security number, a search will provide the most current addresses used by the subject.

Social Security Locator---a search for a social security number for a particular subject can be conducted.

Address Verification---a search using a given address can be conducted to determine whom the residence is listed to.

Address Verification with Neighbors---a search using a given address can result in the neighbor's names, addresses and telephone numbers being provided.

Geographic Searches---a search can be conducted by the person's name and all matches or similar names, addresses and telephone numbers will be listed. Searching a particular city, state or the nation can do the search.

Telephone Number Listings---if a number is known, a search will identify whom the number is listed to. If a number is needed, the above searches may result in this being obtained.

Dossier Report---this report will check the driver's license records and voter's registration records and provides the addresses and associated information (although it will not provide a driving history). In addition, it will list known relatives, known associates, known vehicles, known telephone numbers, driver's license and voter's registration information on known relatives and similar information, all in a single report.

Vehicle Identification---the records can be searched for any vehicles associated with a particular person.

CASE LOGS/TIME SHEETS

CASE LOG SHEETS:

The case log sheet is designed to allow the file to reflect the hours and expenses expended during an investigation. The information enclosed on the report should include:

1. The investigator's name assigned to the case,
2. The case number assigned by Kelmar (which should be on there in case the sheet gets separated from the file),
3. The client's name
4. The person being investigated,

5. The date of the activity (surveillance, record check),
6. The time in which the investigation activity was initiated,
7. The time in which the investigation activity was discontinued,
8. The number of hours expended during the activity-broken down in quarter hours (Ex: 2.25 hours),
9. The description of the activity (surveillance, record checks, etc…), and
10. Any mileage expended, or other costs associated with the case.

Although somewhat tedious to keep up-to-date, this is an important part of the investigation as a current log sheet will allow the investigator and supervisor to immediately determine the current costs associated with the case in relation to the amount allotted by the client.

USEFUL FORMS
Chapter Ten

The following forms are an example of those used by my company. You should use these only as an example and try to change and adapt them to your particular needs.

Report Cover Sheet and Disclaimer:

KELMAR & ASSOCIATES

KELLY RIDDLE	Telephone (210) 342-0509
PRESIDENT	Fax (210) 342-0731
2553 JACKSON KELLER, SUITE 200	E-mail: Kelmar@kelmarpi.com
SAN ANTONIO, TX. 78230	Lic. #: C-05785

CLIENT:
REPRESENTATIVE:
SUBJECT:
DATE OF REPORT:

This report is confidential and is solely for the information and use of the client to whom it is addressed. Kelmar and Associates does not guarantee the accuracy or completeness of outside agency records. The background information contained in this report is subject to the limitations imposed by the respective custodians of record and the accuracy of their files at the time of inquiry. The client and/or their representatives has represented to Kelmar and Associates that the information enclosed in this report will be utilized in a lawful and non-violent manner and agrees to hold Kelmar and Associates and their representatives harmless from miss-use of any or all of this information.

Kelmar File No:

The following sheet is completed by the supervisor and is used by the clerical staff for actually typing the client's bill:

BILLING SHEET

CLAIMANT: _____ KELMAR # _____.

Investigator # 1 Hours......._____ hrs. x $ _____ per hour	= $ _____.
Investigator # 2 Hours......._____ hrs. x $ _____ per hour	= $ _____.
Investigator # 3 Hours......._____ hrs. x $ _____ per hour	= $ _____.
Investigator's Travel Time._____ hrs. x $ _____ per hour	= $ _____.

Mileage................................_____ miles x $ _____ per mile = $ _____.
Telephone Expenses... = $ _____.
Video... = $ _____.
Duplication/Copies... = $ _____.
Mailing/Fed-Ex... = $ _____.
Parking.. = $ _____.
Hotel.. = $ _____.
Meals... = $ _____.
Notary.. = $ _____.
Process Service..................._____ (#).. x $ _____ per service = $ _____.
Other.. = $ _____.

Clerical.. = $ _____.
Transcription................._____ hrs. x $ _____ per hour = $ _____.
Subtotal... = $ _____.
Tax...(.0775)....... = $ _____.

TOTAL AMOUNT DUE.. = $ _____.

KELMAR AND ASSOCIATES
CASE INTAKE INFORMATION

CLIENT INFORMATION

CLIENT NAME: _____ . INSURED: _____ .
ADDRESS: _____ . CONTACT: _____ .
CITY/ZIP: _____ . CLAIM #: _____ .
REP   : _____ . D.O.L. _____ .

ASSIGNMENT INFORMATION

___ Activity Check/Surveillance   ___ Past Employment Invest.
___ Hidden Assets Invest.   ___ Background Invest.
___ Locate/Skip Trace Invest.   ___ Subrogation Invest.
___ Criminal/Civil Check   ___ Driver's License Check
Other

SUBJECT INFORMATION

SUBJECT'S NAME: _____ . DOB: _____ .
ADDRESS: _____ . PHONE
. RACE: _____ SEX: _____ .
HEIGHT: _____ WEIGHT: _____ HAIR: ____ .
SOCIAL SEC.#: _____ INJURY: _____ .

SPECIAL CONDITIONS/INFORMATION

VEHICLES: _____ .
DOCTOR & ADDRESS: _____ .
ADDITIONAL INFORMATION:

DATE RECEIVED:	TAKEN BY:	INVESTIGATOR ASSIGNED:

The preceding form is for new cases that our offices receive. The following form is used in each file to keep track of time and expenses:

KELMAR AND ASSOCIATES
INVESTIGATOR'S CASE LOG SHEET

INVESTIGATOR:_____. CASE #:_____
CLIENT:_____. CLAIMANT:_____

DATE	TIME IN / OUT	HOURS	ACTIVITY	MILES	EXP

EXPENSE EXPLAINATION

Cellular Calls 1 2 3 4 5 6 7 8 9 other____. Video: ____ # of
Long Distance 1 2 3 4 5 6 7 8 9 other____. Parking: $____.
Meals @ cost: $_____   Hotel @ cost:_____.
Record Copies @ cost: $_____ Special Supplies: $_____.
Other: _____:

The following form is used as a reminder in case files dealing with interviewing or investigation premise related cases:

INVESTIGATION CHECK-LIST

1. Automobile/Premises:

_____ Statements (all parties)

_____ Obtain Police Report

_____ Witness Statement

_____ Photos of Accident Scene

_____ Photos of Vehicles

_____ Diagram of Accident Scene Location

_____ Medical/Wage Authorization

_____ Check for Skid Marks/evidence

_____ Neighborhood Canvass

_____ Driver's License History

_____ Criminal History Check

_____ Civil History Check

_____ Other:

The following is an example of one of the contracts our offices use:

CONTRACT FOR SERVICES

Kelmar and Associates, Inc., hereby agrees to provide the following person _____
_____
_____ (hereafter called "client") with investigative services as follows:

_____ Surveillance   _____ Background Investigation
_____ Civil History   _____ Criminal History
_____ Dossier Report   _____ Locate/Skip Trace
_____ Other:
˙

Kelmar and Associates agrees to provide the client with a written report, supporting documents, video tape or other relevant information upon completion of the services requested by the client. Kelmar and Associates agrees to initiate the investigation within three (3) working days or at any other date and time mutually agreed upon by the parties involved.

Kelmar and Associates' hourly rate is $50.00, the mileage rate is .35 per mile, and expenses related to the investigation are additional (at cost). The client agrees to these terms and/or to the following terms:

Kelmar and Associates has received a retainer from the client in the amount of ___
_____$_____. The remaining balance is due and payable upon receipt upon completion of the investigation and receipt of the final report by the client. Payment not received within thirty (30) days from the completion of services (final report date) will be assessed a late fee of 12% per month. Should collection and/or legal services be required to obtain the balance due, these costs will be the responsibility of the client.

I _____(client) have read, understood and agree to said contract and hereby agree to retain Kelmar and Associates, Inc. on my behalf on this ____ day of ____ 200_.

_____ . _____ .
         (CLIENT)   Kelmar and Associates

All employees in case of abuse of company equipment sign the following agreement:

EQUIPMENT AGREEMENT

The undersigned does hereby understand that all video and camera equipment, badges and identification cases, computers, or other equipment furnished by Kelmar and Associates is entrusted to the investigator for the sole benefit of Kelmar and Associates. The undersigned does also understand that all equipment which is mishandled, abused, or damaged due to the undersigned's negligence will result in the repairs or replacement thereof being deducted from the employee's payroll. In addition, any or all equipment lost or stolen while in the possession of the under-signed will be replaced by withholding the amount from the employee's payroll. If insurance coverage applies, the employee may be only subject to reimbursement of the deductible or other costs not covered by the insurance carrier.

The following is an agreement that employees sign regarding cellular telephone use:

TELEPHONE AGREEMENT

The undersigned does hereby acknowledge that Kelmar and Associates is providing a cellular/ digital telephone to the undersigned for use while working for Kelmar and Associates. It is understood that the telephone is being provided for the benefit of Kelmar and Associates as an aid in better work production.

The undersigned understands that the telephone service plan provides for 100 minutes of airtime before additional charges are incurred. It is agreed that the undersigned can use the telephone for personal calls, however, the total airtime for any one-month is to be less than 100 minutes unless extenuating circumstances exist.

The undersigned agrees that personal telephone calls are subject to being withheld from the undersigned's payroll/expense check should personal calls become excessive. It is agreed between both parties that no charges shall apply to the undersigned as long as the total business and personal airtime remains under 100 minutes per month.

_____.   _____.
          Undersigned   Date

Unit # Assigned:

The following is a form used for logging vehicle repossession attempts:

AUTO REPOSSESSIONS

Investigator:_____.

Date Received: _____.

Date Completed; _____.

1. Wrecker:

<u>Vehicle Locate Attempts:</u>

Date:

Date;

Date:

Date:

Date:

Date:

Date:

Vehicle taken to: _____.

The following is a form used for keeping up with video obtained:

VIDEO LOG SHEET

DVD #	DATE OF VIDEO	CASE #	CLAIMANT
1.			
2.			
3.			
4.			
5.			
6.			
7.			
8.			
9.			
10.			
11.			
12.			
13.			
14.			

The following is a form used for requesting medical information primarily on insurance related cases:

AUTHORIZATION FOR MEDICAL & WAGE INFORMATION

I hereby authorize any doctor, hospital, surgeon, dentist, nurse, ambulance owner, insurance company or rehabilitation/convalescent facility to give all of the medical information in their possession concerning the injuries, medical history, treatment and past, present and future condition pertaining to myself to _____ or their representatives.

I authorize any firm or employer to give _____, or their representatives any information concerning the history and nature of my employment, wages, lost time from work, working hours, benefits or payable and the names of any insurance carriers with which I have filed a claim for benefits.

The information furnished will be used in verification, evaluation and negotiation as well as in pertinent legal matters with respect to my claim.

This authorization shall remain valid for the duration of the claim and a Photostat copy shall serve in its stead.

I understand that a copy of this authorization will be furnished to myself or my legal representative on request.

This is not a release of claim for damages.

_____.   _____.
              Signature   Date

KELMAR AND ASSOCIATES
INVESTIGATOR'S WEEKLY LOG

INVESTIGATOR: _____ WEEK: _____ thru _____ x

CASE # OTHER EXPENSE	TOTAL SURV. NUMBER	ADMIN./VIDEO/ HOURS	TOTAL REPORT HRS	EXPENSE HOURS	CELLULAR

AMOUNT DUE INVESTIGATOR

TOTAL MILES: _____ x _____ PER MILE = $_____	
SPECIAL MILES: _____ x _____ PER MILE = $_____	
	TOTAL EXPRNSES: _____
	TOTAL CELLULAR: _____
TOTAL EXPENSES: _____	
TOTAL # OF HOURS: _____ x $_____ PER HOUR = $ LABOR	

The preceding form is used for each investigator to keep track of their time and expenses on a weekly basis for accounting purposes.

INTERNET AND SEARCH ENGINE MARKETING
Chapter Eleven

Marketing in general has seen a transition from print to internet marketing. The face-to-face, personable element of advertising is lacking in this type of element. Additionally, marketing private investigations has some added unique characteristics that do not fit nicely into the "Marketing 101 Basic" courses often taught in college. You must look at your entire marketing campaign and insure that it all compliments other aspects. In the process, you are "branding" your company image. That concept comes easy for me since I am from Texas where branding livestock has been done since the 1800's. Ultimately you want everything that someone sees to point to your company name and logo. Sometimes this will be subtle and other times it will almost scream.

Once you develop a logo, this will appear on your business cards, letterhead, brochures, envelopes, and potentially on pens, hats, calendars, shirts, cups, coffee mugs and other items you may use in your marketing plan. It will most definitely appear on your website. For this reason your logo has to be one that will carry over from item to item. You should have your designer supply it to you in various sizes, resolutions and positions (lateral or vertical). Unfortunately most PI's do not pay near enough attention to their logo and this is such an important part of your name branding. One of the most recognizable names and related logo, although fictional, is "007" and "James Bond." The logo of the gun encompassed in the 007 is recognizable worldwide.

Nothing else has to be said once you see either of these logos. You know exactly who it represents. Other brands that bring the same instant recognition include the "golden arches," the brown delivery truck and brown uniform, the "longhorn" silhouette and other similar symbols. While most people will not have the money to invest in marketing that it took for these to become recognizable globally, you need to start in your "pond" with the mindset of branding your logo on a larger scale.

The logo is extremely important but just as important is the name that you select for your company. "The right name is an advertisement in itself."[40] Few give this the thought process truly deserved for such an important decision. Many investigators simply name their company "John Doe Investigations." While this is the obvious, it most likely is not the best for long range growth. If you name the company after you, any attempts at selling your company down the line will be dramatically decreased. A company without the company's name sake is somewhat odd. To look forward towards growing and eventually selling your company, you should try to have a corporate presence in the name you select. In doing so, it doesn't matter if John Doe is the owner of the company because "Investigations for Today" can be comprised of anyone. It simply makes for a better transition.

There are the pros and cons of using your name for your business name. The main advantage is it gives a personal touch by associating the business with the owner. A personal name is only good for the local area that the name may be known but limits expanding into other geographic areas. With any company name you will have to obtain the internet domain name (name of website). Using your personal name may be too long and using initials may be too short. It is important to have a name that can easily be remembered and found on the internet. Even if it is easily remembered but very long, people may become frustrated by all of the typing. If you are a female and you get divorced, this may also affect your company name if you used your personal name.

Another consideration would be to obtain the domain (website address) for you personally such as www.Kellyriddle.com. If someone is looking to hire you they can always search by your name. You can have as many domain names as you want and have them all point to a single website or multiple sites. Having the

---

[40] Claude Hopkins

domain for your personal name, in addition to your company name, is just another way to market, makes it easier for people to find you and gives you additional key names for search engines.

Once you have your company name and logo, you can begin the process of setting up your website and social media. I would recommend that you go through one of the larger domain name providers such as Network Solutions or Go Daddy. You can search to see if a domain name is available on their websites and if it is, purchase the same. Don't waste your time creating your logo or anything else until you obtain the domain name. Once you have secured the name, you can also have one of these companies host (or park) your website on their server. They have templates that you can use to create a website. However, I strongly suggest you hire a professional web designer. This is your "look" and reputation. Anyone coming to your site will size your company up within the first 10 seconds so good impressions are a must. I would suggest that you use one of the larger companies for hosting your site. At one point I had all my websites being hosted by a friend who has a marketing company. About every six months our domain was getting "black-balled" for spam. Come to find out, anyone with a website on his server had this problem because he sent out a ton of marketing emails and people reported him for emailing spam. When your site gets black-balled, you can't send emails and you may not know this until you recognize that no one is answering your emails. It is a real hassle to get your domain off the black-balled list.

When you get your domain name for your company, you should also set up emails with the same domain name. For example, for XYZinvestigations.com, you would have emails like John@XYZinvestigations.com. This looks more professional than John@aol.com. I would suggest that you set an email up for info@XYZinvestigations.com and use this for inquiries stemming from your site. Add more domain emails for your staff. In doing so, this will give you a more professional look.

Creating an atheistically pleasing website is important as visual appeal will attract and help keep the person on your site. The day of reading large sums of text are gone for the most part. People browse articles, emails and websites so you need to refrain from placing paragraph after paragraph of "dry" content. Short, bullet-point type content will prevail and be the best method for getting key data across to potential clients. On the flip side are websites that are just too busy.

They have information and graphics scattered all over the page like a shotgun sprayed it on the page. There truly is an art to creating the perfect website with the perfect balance of text, graphics and information.

Websites that Work:

-*Project the Right Image* – The site has to be professional, tasteful and appealing. While doing so, the site must represent you and your company in the manner most likely to project a positive outlook.

-*Use Key and Meta Tags* – A website designer is acutely aware that key terminology and "meta tags" are the behind the scene elements that cause search engines to pick up on your website and move them up the placement ladder. These are the terms that people would type into a search engine while trying to locate a private investigator. These are words like "private investigator", "missing persons", "cheating spouse", "surveillance" and similar terms. You must tastefully build them into the text on the front page of your website.

-*Be Careful of Plagiarism and Copyright Infringements* – As part of your market research, you will most likely visit other websites posted by your competitors and other investigators. Even if you find information and graphics that you absolutely love, be careful of plagiarism and copyright infringements. I have known of at least three instances where a PI copied either all or part of another investigator's website. If you design the site yourself, and I do not recommend this, be careful where and how you get the graphics for your site. Website designers normally purchase photographs and graphics to use on your site and you should therefore be free of this issue.

-*Contract for Services on Site* – I have found that posting a contract for services on my website for potential clients to review helps to speed the intake process. If they are shopping and budget is an issue, they can immediately identify our hourly rate. Should our rate be an issue, we have just saved our staff a needless waste of time since they will not be able to afford our services. If the budget is not an issue, we are one-step closer to getting a new client.

-*Why You and Not Your Competitor?* – One of the key questions that many sites often overlook is why the potential client should choose you over a competitor. This goes to the heart of your reputation and should be something you already have an answer for that you can quickly recite to potential clients. If you have done any telephone or face-to-face marketing, you should already have tackled this and a short 2-3 line response should flow readily.

-Display Your Expertise – If you have any expertise or experience that helps separate you from the crowd be sure to include this on your website. Many PI's post things like "former law enforcement" or "retired FBI." However, if you have been given any acclamations or have any specific expertise related directly to the PI profession, be sure to post this to further your professional presentation.

-Media Interview and Articles – Another way that search engines pick-up on your site and move you up the search engine ladder is through short media video clips. If you have written or have had any articles related to your or your company in newspapers, business journals or magazines, be sure to post those on your site as well. Each of these helps present you as a professional while increasing your internet presence.

-Social media links – You should have a company presence on Facebook, Twitter, MySpace and other social media publications. Be sure to post a link to these on your website for potential clients to follow while at the same time increasing your search engine placement.

Search Engine Placement

Once you have a website you can just sit back and wait for all the customers to come in, right? Absolutely incorrect and you have just crossed the first hurdle to internet advertising. Think of all of the millions of websites on the internet and then come to the realization that somehow you have to get potential customers directed to your website. This is done in various ways including your marketing materials such as brochures, newsletters, letterhead, business cards and anything else you might hand out in the course of business. This is considered direct marketing and is targeted towards existing clients or those who have reached out and inquired about your services through word of mouth or in response to receiving one of these items. However, the person sitting at home surfing the internet has to be directed to your website. This is done through search engine optimization (SEO). If you followed the previous instructions and have the correct items included in your website (meta tags, etc…) then you are heading in the right direction.

Search engine placement is a huge industry within the internet and marketing profession. There are numerous ways to insure that your website is included on the first page of a search engine. One is through *"Keyword Management Pay-Per-Click."* A marketing company will literally buy keywords from each of the larger respective search engines and "guarantee" the ranking of specific keywords and the number of traffic generated to your website. You only pay for traffic that sees your web site (the ones that used the keywords selected). For example, if you live in Atlanta, you may want to specify they buy "Atlanta private investigator" as well as similar terms. You need to target the keywords so you are not wasting clicks on investigators in Miami.

One of the problems with the pay-per-click" method is you will get charged every time a person clicks on your placement that is listed on a search engine. If a person is shopping around and they keep coming back to your site through various search engines, you get charged each time. You also have to be careful that you are not being charged for each page they view within your website. If you have ten pages on your site, you may be charged for each page that a single viewer sees while on your site. Should a competitor find your site and realize you are doing a pay-per-click, they could keep hitting your site just to drive up your marketing budget. In the pay-per-click method, you have to set a dollar amount you are willing to spend on your marketing campaign each month. If it is reached on the 15th of the month, you are finished until the 1st of the month rolls around and your budget is refreshed. There are pros and cons with this type of method but this is one where you truly need to tread lightly until you fully understand your return on investment.

Another type of search engine optimization is similar to the pay-per-click but is based on algorithms. In this method, the marketing company's system watches the algorithms of the internet and can use your budget more wisely by increasing the purchase of keywords based on the increased traffic on the internet. It is much like the stock market method of buying low and selling high. When the system recognizes that there is an increase in searches for keywords for your specific geographic area, the money is automatically released to buy the keywords to insure you are at the top of the search engines. Again this requires you to establish a budget to allow the marketing company's software to pull from throughout the month.

Most private investigators do not have a marketing budget when first starting their business. For those in this category, you can do some of the search engine optimization placement yourself. There are free search engine placement websites that you can use for this purpose. There is also free software that you can download and use on a monthly basis. These free software programs require you to enter your website domain name, list the keywords and allows you to save the information for monthly updates. Some of these programs will search your website and pull the keywords off of your site automatically. Understand that you should only submit your website once per month as search engines will start to reject your submission out of suspicion that it is a spamming site. Often many of the search engines will send you a responding email that requires you to confirm your submission. This requires you to simply click on each link within the email.

One of the issues with any type of search engine optimization program is that they often do not submit to the bigger search engines like Yahoo, Google, Bing, etc. These search engines require you to submit your website manually. Of course since these are the bigger search engines, you certainly want to follow through in this area. You can often locate where to do this by going to the bottom of the search engine page and looking under advertising.

Tracking Internet Results

Tracking the results of your on-line marketing will help you determine if your return on investment is working properly. As an example, Yellow Pages (YP.com) provide monthly reports like the one below. It will show you the number of clicks to your site and the key words that were searched to find your site.

Account Performance Report for the previous month

Visitors to your site ⇨ 33
(clicks)

Top Keywords ⇨ security systems & services
(descending order)   spy cameras
                        private investigators
                        kelmar & associates
                        surveillance equipment & services
                        investigation companies
                        investigation service
                        gps tracking for cars
                        covert spy cameras
                        private investigation

Other sites like Google Trends provide historical data and graphs that provide industry specific search terms that enable you to target your search terms:

Google Trends:

private investigations
Search term

+ Add time range

Interest over time

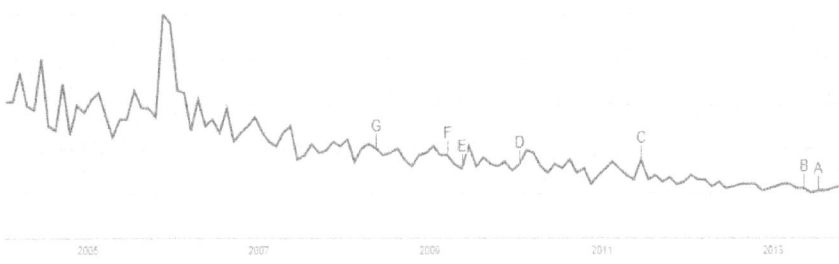

Regional interest

Regional interest

	Region	City
United States	100	
Australia	83	
Netherlands	73	
Canada	73	
United Kingdom	61	
Italy	53	
Spain	31	

Top		Rising	
private investigator	100	dire straits lyrics	Breakout
investigators	60	florida private investigations	Breakout
private investigators	60	private detectives	Breakout
private investigation	40	private investigations license	Breakout
lyrics private investigations	30	private investigations tab	Breakout
private detective	20	private investigator jobs	Breakout
private investigations jobs	15	private investigator license	Breakout
Embed		Embed	

Other areas of Internet marketing:

Social media[41] is a great method to help you expand your company's marketing program and increase customer awareness. There are a number of different types of Social media including Facebook, LinkedIn and Twitter. Social media is interactive and you can sneak up on people by providing a variety of topics that are entertaining while fulfilling the underlying goal of marketing your company. Some of the different forms of social media that you may want to use include:

• *Blogging* – A great deal of people do not understand blogging in reference to marketing. Blogging to post informative information that your niche market or potential customers would find valuable is the key to using this type of media. Consider what things would be interesting and entertaining. Do not just blog every thought as people will start to dismiss your blogs due to shear volume. You

---

[41] http://businessknowledgesource.com

can also use your blog to post videos that you create or you can choose to do a live stream radio or podcast. Look at other blogs to help you determine what type of information is out there and what information you need to add or change in order to provide your niche market with more value.

• *Twitter* – Many businesses are using Twitter in order to market their business but you can only send out short bits of information. With Twitter, you have 140 characters that you can use and your thoughts therefore must be more succinct. It will allow you to post information that must be engaging and informative in order to get your customers to re-tweet the information. The key goal is to have your tweet passed on as it will be able to gain more exposure and you can start increasing your sales by getting a large number of contacts to work with.

• *Facebook* – Is the" social media site at the moment and is focused more on relationships. Facebook took over and surpassed MySpace at the number one social media site. You are not limited by character restraints and can more freely talk and create stronger relationships with your customers. With Facebook you can also post several pictures and videos for your customers.

• *Email* – This is still considered a form of social networking as you have a chance to keep in touch with your customers. You can use emails to send out great information like newsletters to your customers and information updates. You can also start writing articles and offering a small paragraph of information in the email in order to get people to click on the link. Again, I would suggest you use a Yahoo, Gmail or other account that is not tied your domain name to keep your email and domain from being placed on the spam black lists.

• *Webinars* – A great way to connect with your customers is to offer webinars for training and to discuss hot topics. This is an interactive way for customers to ask your company questions and for you to offer them educational information and more insight into your company.

• *Video streams* – Posting video streams on your website can be a useful tool if done professionally. You can provide media interviews, short infomercials or anything else entertaining.

• *Apps* – You may create apps that can be used for the business but this is the toughest of all the social media marketing tools. An app must provide some type of useful information or on-line access. An app that simply states information about your company will be rejected by the app store.

• *Stand out from the crowd* - There are a huge amount of choices for consumers so you will have to make sure that you are using social media networking in a manner that will help your business to stand out from the competition. You can do this by being creative and innovative. Remember, that you only have a few seconds to attract and keep the attention of your potential customers.

• *Offer something of value* - If you are simply using social media networking to aggressively promote your business, chances are that your readers will soon tire of your constant promotion and move on. You need to make sure that you are offering your customers something of value. You can do this by actively engaging in whatever social media networking you choose. If someone asks you a question, then answer it, if you put out a Tweet, make sure that your customers will want to read what you have offered, and finally, be helpful and supportive.

• *Be patient with your social media networking efforts* - You may not get the overwhelming response that you think you will as soon as you start using social media sites. You need to be patient and let this type of business promotion work. If you have correctly positioned yourself on the social media networking site, the word will spread and more and more customers will seek you out. However, you have to remember, that this most likely will take some

- *Be polite* – Just like typing with all capital letters which is construed as yelling, everything you do on social media networking must be polite. Nothing can turn off potential customers more than being rude and being a bully. You want to make sure that everything you put on your social media networking sites is polite, courteous, and helps others. If you receive criticism on social media site, you need to take it in stride and if you respond, do so in a positive and proactive manner.

Following are 5 tips on how you can build a successful social media business.

Tip # 1 – Research!

Like any marketing program you are planning to start you need to do your research and to completely understand what you are getting yourself into. It is a good idea to sign up for your account and to really monitor other companies on the social media platform to see what they are doing. It helps you to gain insight into how the social media site works and what type of information will really drive conversations on it. As you research this information you can then start participating in it and start sending out engaging messages to your followers.

Tip # 2 – Create a Marketing Agenda

Before you start sending out random postings you need to determine what your ultimate goal is. You have to define the goals because it does make it much easier for you to build relationships with your customers and to start creating programs that will build loyalty with the customers as well. Create a list of your goals first and you will find that it is much easier for you to focus on them properly when you start using social media sites.

Tip # 3 – What will your account be?

You need to set up your profile and specify what type of account it will be such as a hybrid account, personal account, or a company account? Creating the right type of account in the beginning will make it much easier for you to focus properly with your social media account. The branding profiles are nice if you want to do a lot of contests or offer industry news but if you are looking for building relationships with the customers, focus more on your business account. A guideline to remember with postings is to abide by the 80/20 rule. This means that 80% of your postings will be industry related and the other 20% can be conversational.

Tip # 4 – Build trust and credibility

Why do people follow others social media sites? They want to see a company that has been able to build trust with them and has also made a presence in their community. It is important that you use your account to post credible information so that you can build trust and credibility with your customers. Engage your customers and be personable with them in order to gain the right type of information from them and to create trust with the customers.

Tip # 5 – Learn

As you play around with social media and start to become successful with it you need to really take a step back and learn from it. You want to track and measure the results that come in with from social media accounts and really use this information to your advantage to generate more leads.

There is a lot more to social media than tweets and status updates. If you are going to put together a social media strategy to build your business, it is important to embrace the diversity and complexity of social media and utilize the various tools available to you. The following is a look at valuable tools in your social media arsenal:

Social Bookmarking – This is going to help you stay on top of relevant content, and help build your brand and customer awareness. Some of the best social bookmarking sites include StumbleUpon and Delicious. These will help you to have real insight into the social aspect of your industry and what interests your target market.

Social Aggregation – This is a huge tool because it allows you to maintain social network profiles, blog profiles, video sharing sites, image sites and other relevant profiles all in one convenient location. Again, if you are using several social media sites, this is a great way to aggregate them and maintain your connections on all. Great services for this include: FriendFeed, Lifestyle.fm and MyBlogLog. If you intend to have a successful social media campaign an aggregate service is very useful. It will help you stay aware of your follower's activity, fans, friends, etc. and not let anything relevant or important fall through the cracks in your effort to maintain several profiles.

Micro Blogging – These are the tools like Twitter, where you post micro blogs such as status updates, etc. where you stay involved in the community activity with short posts. It is a popular form of keeping in contact and relevant in your industry.

Video Production and Syndication – Social media means all kinds of media, this means video blogs, video tutorials, and more. The production of, optimization of, and syndication of video to popular video sharing sites, such as YouTube is a critical component of a social media campaign.

Learning to use the social media tools available to you will help you create a more effective social media campaign. In addition, learn to track, measure, and define the parameters of your social media tactics.

Marketing on the internet can be a full-time job but you can get proficient in this area by spending some quality time performing this activity on a regular basis. Like any type of marketing plan, it will only work if you are consistent and maintain a presence. You should also explore other options for marketing your services on the internet including:

-*Geographic Specific Sites* – Wherever you live, there are local television and radio stations that have their own websites. You should research their advertising prerequisites to determine if this is a fit for your budget and audience. There are also sites that are geared towards tourism and conventions for your local area. If someone is looking for a PI in your area to watch their spouse who is traveling to attend a convention, this may be the perfect site to find your company.

-*Private Investigation Trade Sites* – Each of the state and national private investigation associations have their own respective websites and most have the opportunity to advertise on these and/or increase your individual listings under "find an investigator." In addition, there are organizations like PI Now, the PI Magazine, Pursuit Magazine and similar avenues you may consider.

In today's business climate, the internet is the perfect marketing venue for any business. To be effective, you need to encompass a good website along with search engine placement, social media sites, blogs and the full range of tools that are available.

EFFECTIVE BUSINESS PLANS
Chapter Twelve

A business plan is an absolute must for anyone considering going into business or who currently is in business. I wrote my first business plan within the first year of being in business and it help to focus my thoughts, set my course and project the future. I can honestly state that the projections outlined 25 years ago have come to pass almost verbatim. No matter how big or small you think you want your business to be, a business plan will help target your thoughts.

According to Alyssa Gregory[42] in Small Business Administration, the following reasons are why you should have a business plan:

A Business Plan is Simply a Must-Have for Some Businesses

If you plan to approach a financial institution for a loan, apply for a **small business grant**, pitch your business idea to investors, or enlist the support of a business partner, a business plan is required.

Potential investors and supporters want to see the true potential of your business idea clearly laid out in hard facts and numbers. A business plan is the best, and generally, the only acceptable way to provide this information.

A Business Plan Helps You Make Decisions

There are some sections in a traditional business plan that you simply cannot complete if you are on the fence, undecided, or not fully committed to a certain point. Business plans help you eliminate the gray area because you have to write specific information down in black and white. Making tough decisions is often one of the hardest and most useful parts of writing a business plan.

For example, if you have not decided on exactly what products you will sell at what price points, it will be very difficult for you to complete the **Products and Services Section** of your business plan. Identifying this and other vital information is a valuable end product of the business planning process.

A Business Plan Can Be a Reality Check

---

[42] http://sbinformation.about.com/od/businessplans

Writing a business plan is often the first real struggle for the small business owner who wants to launch a new venture, but doesn't want to consider that his or her business idea may be a bit flawed or is not yet fully developed.

While this is an unwelcome and terrifying thought for an impassioned entrepreneur, identifying gaps early on in the process gives business owners a chance to shore up their research, test their ideas and take steps to make the business stronger and more viable. This may initially be a step back, but any and all further work can bolster the entrepreneur's chance of success before he or she invests time and money in a business that is likely to fail.

A Business Plan Can Give You New Ideas

Discovering new ideas, different approaches and fresh perspectives are some of best things that can happen from the depths of the business planning process. Despite the sometimes negative reputation, a business plan isn't just a long, stiff, and structured document.

In fact, an effective business plan is the opposite; it's a flexible, growing and dynamic tool that can help you think creatively and come up with new solutions for some of your toughest business challenges. This is especially true when you consider the **Marketing Strategy Section**. Here, as you create a blueprint for your marketing activities, creativity and fresh ideas are invaluable.

A Business Plan Creates an Action Plan

A business plan is a useful document for any small business owner. But when you use your business plan as a tool to help you outline action items, next steps and future activities, you are creating a living, breathing document that not only outlines where you are and where you want to be, but also gives you the directions you need to get there.

The following is an example of the first business plan I wrote for my company and dealt with where we were at that time and the projected expansion plans. Initially Kelmar conducted 100% insurance related investigations and this has changed to only about 25% of our business model.

BUSINESS OVERVIEW

SUMMARY:

    Kelmar and Associates is a private investigation company that has been in business since April of 1989. The enclosed prospectus has been prepared for confidential use by potential investors. Kelmar and Associates intends to capture the market through the following methods:

1. Expansion of the investigative and consulting offices
2. Expansion of training through the "The PI Institute of Education" for the industry and general public
3. Creating small stores under the name of "PI Gadgets" linked to offices that will sale PI products to the industry and general public
4. Creating an on-line catalog for PI products sold in the PI Gadget stores
5. Creating a source for temporary investigators, consultants and undercover operatives through the "PI Temps."
6. Integrating the investigative business, the PI school, the PI stores and the PI Temps into a complete business that will cycle clients and customers from one business entity to the other.

Kelmar and Associates intends to open 13-14 office locations and expand from East to West Coast initially. After sufficient profit has been realized, an additional 10-12 offices will be added to fully expand the operation into a nationwide organization. It is anticipated that the entire operation will be complete and profitable within the 3-4 year time table.

    In addition to expanding the private investigation business, the company intends to utilize their private investigation school, "The PI Institute of Education," to further market the business and to provide a source of investigators for the "PI Temps." The company intends to provide a source for temporary investigators, consultants and undercover operatives through the PI Temps.

    The initial investment will be utilized to support salaries for the new offices, to add a full-time marketing representative, to dramatically increase advertising in the new office locations and to purchase equipment. A full time instructor will be hired for the PI School as well as a full time executive for the PI Temps. Capital will also be needed and utilized to purchase inventory for the PI stores. Long term goals include positioning the company on the stock market to realize the greatest potential for investors.

As most professions, the private investigation profession has created an atmosphere in which specialization in a specific area is required. Because of prior experience and contacts in the insurance industry, Kelmar and Associates specializes in private investigations for the insurance industry and their attorneys. The typical insurance claims office is responsible for large geographic areas, which may include up to 10-15 States. It has become obvious that a private investigation company, specializing in insurance investigations, should be able to expand and maintain offices in key areas to service these geographic needs. At the present time, insurance adjusters are required to take a chance on small, unknown companies or rely on national *security guard* companies which conduct investigations as a side-line.

The owner of Kelmar and Associates has been designated an expert in five different specialties that has allowed the company to become more diversified. Although insurance investigations is a major part of the company's income, additional areas of expertise has allowed the company to expand the potential for profit. Expansion in these areas will also be targeted to increase the profit margins of the company.

Kelmar and Associates has become a significant supplier of private investigations for the insurance industry in the Central and South Texas areas. The company intends to expand their geographic coverage by adding 10-13 new offices to increase their market presence and dominate the insurance investigation industry in the South. New offices will be added in the geographic areas known to be regional and/or district offices for insurance companies. Business in the new offices will be generated initially from the pre-existing clients. In addition, Kelmar intends to include new industry development and the expansion of other services to compliment the strong surveillance product currently being offered. The company proposes to seek investors and board members to support and assist in this development. It is anticipated that the company will need approximately $1.5 million dollars to fully expand and add the divisions required to achieve the stated goals and return a substantial return to the investors.

BUSINESS DESCRIPTION:

Kelmar and Associates is a Chapter "S" Corporation, incorporated in the State of Texas in April of 1989. Kelmar and Associates is a private investigation company specializing in insurance investigations, legal work and corporate investigations. The primary source of generating income is through typical marketing techniques, most of which, is word-of-mouth contacts and trade publications. Although the insurance industry has been the market most heavily targeted, this industry has dropped from 100% of the company's income to approximately 35%. The company has diversified and a major portion of the income now comes from nursing home abuse investigations, corporate investigations and domestic cases. The typical insurance investigation centers around an insurance adjuster making an assignment to Kelmar and Associates for surveillance and/or a background investigation. The insurance adjuster will also make assignments for obtaining recorded statements from witnesses, hidden asset investigations, skip tracing (or locating a particular person), and civil and criminal history checks.

PRODUCT/SERVICE:

Kelmar and Associates provides private investigation services directed primarily at the corporate world. Approximately ninety 40 percent (40%) of the cases assigned to Kelmar involve surveillance with the primary goal being to obtain documentation that either supports or refutes the alleged injury of an individual. At the completion of the surveillance, a written report, invoice, video documentation and related records are provided to the client. The information that is obtained by Kelmar allows our clients to better understand the subject and their situation. This in turn, provides the client with the proper information in which to make informed business decisions.

Over the eleven years that Kelmar has been conducting investigations, surveillance has remained one of the primary services and sources of income. Background investigations, pre-employment checks, and related background searches have been a fluctuating source of income.

Due to the prior experience of Mr. Riddle, Kelmar and Associates also conducted automobile and property damage appraisals for several insurance companies. This was done primarily as an attempt to help stabilize the financial picture of the company for the first two years. However, the three insurance companies which referred this type of work to Kelmar have since moved out of the Texas insurance market. In addition, the determination had already been made to phase out the appraisals as the service was creating identification problems with some clients only being aware that the company conducted appraisals and not investigations. The insurance adjusters appeared to have a difficult time identifying Kelmar with both services and markets. The company has been able to survive and grow in the unstable economic conditions of the 1980's and early 1990's and has evolved into a stable and growing organization.

ADDITIONAL SERVICES:

The PI Institute of Education:

Mr. Riddle is also the *Founder of the PI Institute of Education*, which was created to provide continuing education to investigators in Texas after the State Board of PI's initiated the requirement in 1997. Classes are taught the last Friday and Saturday of each month in the corporate offices of Kelmar and Associates. A three month course has already been compiled and expansion of the school to the general public will be pursued. Kelmar and Associates is currently seeking approval to accept grant and GI Bill income to further enhance the market of this school. Additionally, the 9 books and 4 video tapes that Mr. Riddle has already written will be turned into correspondence courses that can be obtained via the company's web site. The investigators of Kelmar and Associates will also continue to attend the school, which will also be used as a marketing tool to demonstrate the professionalism of the company's investigators.

The school will be used to provide a source for temporary investigators, undercover operatives and consultants throughout the industry, which will be marketed through the PI Temps. The students will complete 40 hours of education and training at a cost expected to be $599 per student. After completing the course, the student will be licensed under Kelmar and Associates and will be available to assignments through the PI Temps. *Note:* Investigators have to be licensed by the state board and can only be licensed by one agency at a time. This will therefore assist in keeping students and consultants tied to the company and PI Temps.

PI Temps:

It has been determined that a need exists within the industry to provide temporary investigators, consultants and undercover operatives to understaffed agencies. According to information obtained from the trade organization, The

Global Investigator's Network, 83% of the PI agencies are 1-2 person operations. Due to this fact, the agencies often find themselves in a situation where they need temporary investigators to provide surveillance or investigative services to clients. However, due to the fear of competitors learning an agency's clientele list, many will not bring in other competitor's employees. With this in mind, an agency specifically geared towards providing contract employees in a non-competitive atmosphere is anticipated to be well received. Additionally, training and licensing is a major issue. Through the PI Institute of Education, the candidates will receive the necessary training, followed by licensing under Kelmar and Associates. Due to the fact that an investigator can only be licensed by one agency at a time, direct control and loyalty to Kelmar and PI Temps is anticipated.

Additional Investigative Services:

Kelmar and Associates has demonstrated the ability to conduct professional surveillances to our existing clients. However, additional services will be more actively marketed and pursued for both the existing clients and new industries. Although some of these services are currently being conducted by Kelmar, a more aggressive approach will be taken to acquire a larger share of the market relating to these services. These additional surveillances will include:

* <u>Nursing Home Abuse:</u> Mr. Riddle has become the only investigator to author a book and video on this topic and has therefore been designated an expert in these types of cases. The legal profession is identifying this as the wave of the future due to the increase in awareness, the lack of background investigations on employees and the increasing number of people reaching the age for elder care. Kelmar and Associates currently derives approximately 40% of their income from these types of investigations and this appears to be increasing. Mr. Riddle has already dealt with 20/20, Dateline, 60 Minutes and other T.V. shows related to this topic, which further enhances the company's position in the industry related to these cases.

* <u>Corporate Investigations:</u> Kelmar and Associates has been successful in providing investigations for defending sexual harassment lawsuits, hostile take-overs, misappropriation of trade secrets and related investigations. Due to our success in these areas, this portion of the business continues to show an increase.

* <u>Criminal Investigations:</u> Kelmar and Associates intentionally refrained from conducting criminal investigations until late 1997. However, high profile

cases such as the Mexican Mafia cases were handled by the company. Due to the successful handling of these and other cases, additional criminal investigations have been assigned and continued growth in this area is expected.

* Surveillance: Although surveillance is currently the strongest service offered by Kelmar, the company intends to expand their efforts in this area to industries not currently using the standard mobile surveillance. This would include in-store anti-theft surveillance, compound surveillance for large industrial sites, workplace sexual harassment surveillance and security/protection surveillance. Each major industry has a particular need that can be filled through proper surveillance techniques (Ex: surveillance to deter theft, pilferage, and mishandling of baggage by the airlines or surveillance for drug usage among employees). A more aggressive marketing approach will be taken to acquire a segment of these additional industries.

* Background Checks: Kelmar currently provides limited background checks and are usually in conjunction with a surveillance assignment. The company will pursue this type of investigation more aggressively, especially outside of the insurance industry. School districts, Churches, daycares and similar organizations who are charged with the care of children have increasingly become more susceptible to employees engaging in child molestation and the resulting large monetary settlements. Background checks in these areas will be actively pursued as well as pre-marital background checks and similar areas.

* Pre-Employment Checks: Due to the increase in embezzlement, sexual harassment, child molestations, drug and alcohol abuse and related problems, all employers are becoming increasingly aware of their liability regarding this type of conduct in the work force. These types of investigations have played a limited role in the over-all picture of Kelmar and Associates thus far. However, additional measures will be implemented to address these issues and to pursue those employers in need of this service.

* Pre-Marital Checks: Kelmar has obtained some success in the marketing of this service and will increase efforts to address this type of investigation for the general public. Domestic investigations are a specialized area of private investigations that Kelmar has purposely limited their exposure to due to numerous liabilities not present in other types of investigations. However, divorce/domestic cases will be more actively pursued with a continued cases-by-case evaluation before accepting this type of assignment.

* <u>Hidden Asset Investigations:</u>   Although the insurance industry utilizes Kelmar and Associates in this area to discover assets in which the insurance company could recover their losses, this type of investigation has many applications outside the insurance industry. Kelmar provided a tremendous amount of this type of service to banks and savings and loans until the savings and loan industry's problems. Pursuit of this type of investigation dramatically declined due to the Federal Law Enforcement's involvement in the industry and the spending of the savings and loans being scrutinized. This industry again needs to be pursued, as well as businesses involved in possible joint ventures, mergers, acquisitions and similar situations. Kelmar will implement a more aggressive approach to these industries.

* <u>Legal Support:</u>   Although Kelmar currently services some of the largest law firms in the State of Texas, additional strides will be made to increase the amount of law firms utilizing the services of Kelmar. Law firms typically request surveillance, background checks, hidden asset investigations, real estate and property searches and a facet of other investigations that Kelmar intends to pursue.

* <u>Domestic Cases:</u>   Kelmar and Associates intentionally refrained from handling these types of cases initially. However, the company now solicits these types of investigations and have been involved in numerous high-profile cases that have been covered by the media. This is an area of expansion that will continue to be pursued by the company.

* <u>CCTV Installation:</u> Kelmar and Associates currently provide covert and standard closed circuit TV systems for clients attempting to deter theft and false claims. In the year 2000, the company has received approximately $50,000 in revenue generated from these services. The company intends to aggressively market this type of service under the new marketing plan.

By increasing the other types of investigative services and more actively promoting these services to the industries outside of the insurance industry, Kelmar and Associates intends to acquire a larger segment of the overall dollars spent on investigations. However, the insurance industry will continue to be pursued as the number one priority for Kelmar, with the additional services being augmented to provide a more stable, profit centered organization.

MARKETING:

It is acknowledged that marketing is one of the key factors in the success of any organization. The ability to market successfully has been demonstrated by Mr. Riddle being selected as the **#1 PI in the United States** (PI Magazine), the **1997-98 PI of the Year** (National Assoc. of Investigative Specialists) and **One of the Top 25 PI's of the Century** (NAIS). In addition, Mr. Riddle is the author of 9 books, 4 video tapes and an Internet Investigation Software Program that further enhances the prolific nature of the company. Mr. Riddle was a guest lecturer at more than 40 seminars in 1998 alone and has been a lecturer at more than 150 in the past three years. These appearances assist the company in becoming stronger within the industry. Mr. Riddle is a regular columnist for the national trade publication, *The PI Magazine*, which provides further marketing.

Mr. Riddle is also the *Founder of the Association of Christian Investigators*, which has more than 750 members in 43 States and 6 Countries. This non-profit association has further enhanced the credibility and prolific character of Mr. Riddle and Kelmar and Associates.

The *company web site (www.kelmarpi.com)* currently receives more than 13,000 hits per month. Loose evaluation of cases and income derived from this site indicates the company has received approximately $xxxxx each year for the past two years that is directly attributed to the site. This year alone, the company received more than $xxxx from only one case that was obtained through the web site.

Because the owner of Kelmar had prior experience in the insurance industry, contacts were readily generated for Kelmar from word-of-mouth. In addition, insurance adjusters frequently change companies, which increased the market spread of Kelmar through those adjusters who utilized their services at the new insurance company. Typical marketing techniques have been used in the past such as mail-outs, brochures, marketing lunches, telephone cold-calls, etc... A full-time marketing position has not been established up to this point within Kelmar. However, to properly expand and provide the appropriate marketing required, a full-time marketing position is proposed. The individual will be responsible for appearing at insurance claims association functions, bar association functions, Chamber of Commerce events, appropriate social gathering, trade shows for targeted industries, cold-calling and follow-up contacts and related functions. It is anticipated that one additional clerical position will be needed to keep up with the marketing demands and to allow investigators who have generated leads to contact the marketing department for appropriate follow-up.

<u>Books and Products:</u> Although the 9 books and other products produced by Mr. Riddle are anticipated to remain the sole possession of Mr. Riddle, these items will be used to further market the company. Mr. Riddle uses these items to establish his expertise, help gain media attention and are often given away as marketing tools. As new offices are opened, Mr. Riddle will use these to conduct autograph sessions at local bookstores, to gain media attention and to assist in marketing specific industries.

<u>Newsletter:</u> Kelmar and Associates currently publishes a newsletter which is mailed to clients and potential clients every other month. The newsletter will continue to assist in the marketing of new offices, promotion of business and in name recognition.

<u>Seminars:</u> Mr. Riddle has been the guest lecturer at more than 150 conventions and seminars over the past three years. Additional speaking engagements will assist in marketing the services offered by the company. The company currently has a professional booth that is displayed at these engagements. Several new and more encompassing booths will be obtained to further assist in this marketing. It should be understood that each state has at least one trade association, such as the Texas Association of Licensed Investigators that provide ready access to the PI industry. It is expected that the company will also attend other conventions in industries such as the insurance, legal, medical, airlines, etc. to further promote our services.

Upon receipt of venture capital, the company will obtain the services of a full-time marketing expert to assist in the growth of the company.

BOARD OF DIRECTORS:

Kelmar and Associates expects to fill some of the Board of Director positions with the investors or their representatives: However, the following positions are currently anticipated:

<u>Kelly E. Riddle:</u>   Mr. Riddle has more than sixteen years of investigative experience including former law enforcement and employment with two investigative companies before starting Kelmar and Associates. In addition, he

worked in the insurance industry as an adjuster and investigator. Mr. Riddle holds a B.S. degree in Criminal Justice with a minor in Business Administration from the University of N. Alabama.

<u>Joseph O'Connell:</u>   Mr. O'Connell has an extensive educational and employment background which includes more than 20 years with the FBI. Mr. O'Connell retired from the FBI as the Agent in Charge of the San Antonio office and opened his own private investigation company and eventually became manager of the San Antonio office for a separate investigative company.

FINANCIAL HISTORY:

Kelmar and Associates has been in existence for over twenty years and has weathered numerous circumstances to become a strong, aggressive company. Kelmar was originally started by Kelly E. Riddle and Mark F. Jones. The first three letters of each of the partner's first names were combined to establish the name, "Kelmar". Mr. Jones' business interests were bought out in February of 1994 and Kelmar is now owned and operated solely by Mr. Riddle.

Kelmar and Associates survived using the business proceeds to promote a second start-up company, also previously owned by Mr. Jones and Mr. Riddle. After being in business for approximately one year, Mr. Jones had intended to start a second company to conduct research and development and eventually sell a high-technological infrared night vision device. A partnership was generated between Mr. Jones and Mr. Riddle in order to allow the proceeds of the investigation company to support this new start-up company. Mr. Jones spent approximately 85% of his time in this endeavor, which also took a great deal of financial resources from Kelmar and Associates over a four year period. However, as of February of 1994, Kelmar is no longer involved in the support of this company, allowing all resources and energy to be focused solely on the success of Kelmar and Associates.

The company has grossed an average of $xxxxx each year since the inception of the company. The profit/loss ratio is exaggerated towards the negative due to the use of excess income having been used to support the previously mentioned start-up company. Proper attention to Kelmar and Associates has already began to show a promising increase in the company's future income ability.

The performance and typical expenses for Kelmar and Associates is outlined in the following:

1989	$xxxxxxxxxxx
1990	$xxxxxxxxxxx
1991	$xxxxxxxxxxx
1992	$xxxxxxxxxxx
1993	$xxxxxxxxxxx
1994	$xxxxxxxxxxx
1995	$xxxxxxxxxxx
1996	$xxxxxxxxxxx
Etc…	ETC…

EXPANSION OF OFFICES

NEW OFFICE LOCATIONS:

Kelmar will add new offices, when feasible, to accent and augment pre-existing offices and to draw on the current clients that Kelmar services within the insurance industry. As most insurance companies have district and/or regional offices to oversee the claims in a particular state or states, attempts to locate new offices in geographic areas which will accommodate the insurance claims office will be conducted. In addition, site selections will be conducted based on overall economic features of a particular area as related to private investigations. The offices will also be selected based on such factors as weather, which has an effect on the amount of surveillance cases assigned. The ability to provide cross-assignments between all of the offices will also be a factor for selection.

The company will also obtain office space that is suitable for housing a small store front for the "PI Gadget" stores, classroom space for the "PI Institute of Education," and office area for the "PI Temps." This will allow for better supervision and better marketing for all divisions.

The proposed plan is to open 10-13 office operations primarily in the Southern part of the United States and provide East to West coast coverage. After these offices are stable and profitable an additional 10-12 offices will be opened in the Northern United States to provide a total "national" operation. The initial sites which have been selected are as follows and are in the anticipated order in which they will be added:

1. Dallas/Ft. Worth: This particular area has always been a strong regional office area for insurance companies. In addition, the area accommodates some Fortune 100 and Fortune 500 companies and there is a general economic stability in this area.

2. Houston: This area is generally a strong location for the insurance industry regarding worker's compensation and liability cases. Some insurance carriers have decided to distance themselves from the Houston property insurance market due to possible hurricanes. However, the over-all insurance business is strong in Houston and the oil companies are beginning to return from the earlier decade of disruption.

3. McAllen: The Rio Grande Valley has a tremendous influx of population due to Mexico, college students during holidays and "winter-Texans" from northern states during the winter. The Valley has a reputation of being very pro-plaintiff and the insurance companies and employers are striving to turn that around and would therefore be a good location for an office. The NAFTA agreement should also increase the economy in the Valley.

4. El Paso: This City is on the border of Mexico, New Mexico and Texas and has income derived from these areas. Because of the type of populace, this area is known as being high on the priority list of insurance companies and employers. In addition, the NAFTA agreement should increase the economy in the area.

5. Oklahoma City: The first out-of-state office will be close enough to control and is the capital city of Oklahoma. Major businesses and regional insurance offices tend to concentrate around the capital of a state, as is the case in Oklahoma.

6. Little Rock: An office at this location would complement the other offices and allow for easy cross-assignments. Once again, Little Rock is the Capital of Arkansas and is located in the strongest strategic location in the area.

7. Birmingham: Although Birmingham is not the Capital of Alabama, Birmingham has more business presence than Montgomery. In addition, most of the insurance company's regional offices are located in Birmingham.

8. Atlanta: This area is well established with businesses that are stable, is the capital of Georgia, is fairly centrally located in the state and is close enough to the other offices to work well within the organization.

9. Nashville: Once again, Nashville is the capital of Tennessee, is centrally located in the state and is well established with businesses and entertainers. This location should complement the other office locations.

10. Jacksonville: Being in the north part of Florida, assignments may be sought from just across the south borders of Georgia and Alabama and will complement the Atlanta and Birmingham offices. The city is located in a key location in the state, where IH-10 and IH-95 intersect.

11. Orlando and/or Miami: Either of these locations will serve to service the south and central part of Florida and will complement the Jacksonville office. Because of the entertainment industry in this area, as well as the insurance presence, either of these locations would be a good choice. Additional marketing analysis will be conducted before a selection is made.

12. Phoenix: Being the capital of Arizona, being almost center of the state and being bordered by Utah, Colorado, New Mexico, Nevada, California and Mexico will create a golden opportunity to flourish in this office location.

13. Los Angeles: This office would complete an East to West coast organizational structure and provide a culmination of marketing advantages. Several insurance companies have their home offices in Los Angeles, as well as others who have regional offices. Los Angeles has always been a strong financial presence in California and should complement the entire organization.

PROJECTED START-UP COSTS (Investigation Expansion)

Office Setup/Costs:

The idea of obtaining office space that will allow room for the investigation division, along with the PI Temps, the PI Institute of Education and a small store will help alleviate the financial burden on any one division. Opening "offices" in the new areas will require sufficient capital to handle payroll, limited office equipment, purchase inventory for the stores and provide appropriate advertising. The typical investigator will need to have basic equipment on a day to day basis. Other equipment that is more expensive and seldom used or needed will be kept in the home office and available when needed. The equipment and projected costs associated with opening these satellite offices are:

Current Expenses with Anticipated Increases:

Salaries	$xxxxxxx
Taxes - Payroll	$xxxxxxx
Taxes - Property	$xxxxxxx
Taxes - Sales Tax	$xxxxxxx
Taxes - Other	$xxxxxxx
Office Rent	$xxxxxxx
Utilities	$xxxxxxx
Security System	$xxxxxxx
Office Supplies	$xxxxxxx
Maintenance	$xxxxxxx
Equipment	$xxxxxxx
Professional Fees	$xxxxxxx
Postage	$xxxxxxx
Licenses & Permits	$xxxxxxx
Insurance	$xxxxxxx
Dues & Subscription	$xxxxxxx
Advertising Expenses	$xxxxxxx
Janitorial	$xxxxxxx
Bank Charges	$xxxxxxx
Outside Services.	$xxxxxxx

Additional Areas of Anticipated Expense Increases:

Salary (Marketing Position)	$xxxxxxx

Clerical (3 new)	$xxxxxxx
Branch Manager	$xxxxxxx
Comptroller Position	$xxxxxxx
Investigator Positions	$xxxxxxx
Phone/Fax	$xxxxxxx
Postal Expense	$xxxxxxx
Office Supplies	$xxxxxxx
Database Expense	$xxxxxxx
Marketing Related Expenses	$xxxxxxx
Travel/Hotel Expenses	$xxxxxxx
Advertising	$xxxxxxx
Company Vehicle	$xxxxxxx
Vehicle Maintenance	$xxxxxxx
Health Insurance	$xxxxxxx
Liability Insurance	$xxxxxxx

Additional Equipment Expenses:

Video Cameras	$xxxxxxx
DVR	$xxxxxxx
Covert Equipment	$xxxxxxx
Color TV	$xxxxxxx
Computers	$xxxxxxx
Printers	$xxxxxxx
Digital Camera	$xxxxxxx
Digital Audio Recorder	$xxxxxxx
Cell Phone	$xxxxxxx
Office Furniture	$xxxxxxx
Supplies	$xxxxxxx

A good business plan is very much like a good investigation and should detail the "who, what, when, where and why." Who are you, what do you want to become, in what time frame, where do you want to expand and why? If preparing a business plan for a small business loan or for investors, they want to know when they will get their money back and how much money they will make on their loan/investment.

Preparing a business plan requires you to do a "gut check" and determine what you really want out of business. Once you decide that you need to document the plan to get to the stated goal. After writing the plan, it doesn't do any good if you never review the plan. You should measure your progress on a quarterly basis and adjust both the business plan as well as your methods for achieving the stated plan.

Being at the helm of your own business can be extremely rewarding. Failing at business can be extremely devastating both emotionally and financially. If it is worthy of doing, it is worthy of doing right.

RESIDUAL INCOME
Chapter Thirteen

Residual income[43] is also known as passive or recurring income and is different from a regular wage that's based on the number of hours invested in a particular job. Residual income continues to generate itself even after the work has been completed. Such income helps you earn more while working less as it continues to pay recurrently for work done once. There is 24 hours in a day, period - simple math. You can only work a certain number of hours in any given day and you can only do this for a certain number of days in a week or month before you need a break. Residual income allows you to make money in addition to the money earned while working hour to hour and continues to provide an income even while you are sleeping.

As a private investigator, there are only a few ways to earn money. You can work more hours, work more cases or hire others to help work cases so you can increase the volume of cases. The problem with this is it also increases the amount of overhead (labor, expenses, etc...). However, there are ways to achieve both residual income and supplemental income that include:

On-line training – Many state licensing boards require private investigators to obtain continuing education. Setting up a website that offers courses that are approved for continuing education is one method of achieving residual income. You can also market these courses to potential private investigators who are trying to break into the field. The student can take the courses at any time they have access to the internet, regardless of what you are doing at that time.

On-line equipment sales - You can easily set up a pass-through website where you can sell PI equipment without incurring the cost to maintain inventory. There are companies such as Law Mate.com that will assist you in this endeavor. When you get an order, Law Mate fulfills the order, packaging and mailing the order. You collect the money and pay the wholesale fee to Law Mate.

Alarm monitoring – This is a volume driven business. You can contract with a monitoring station in your area. They have the staff, the equipment and will assist you in making your company look like a full-fledged alarm monitoring company.

---

[43] http://www.wahm.com/articles/residual-income.html

You pay the alarm monitoring station a fee (usually $4.95 - $7.95) and then resell the monthly monitoring service for $19.95 - $34.95. There are local wholesale equipment providers where you can set up an account to purchase the alarm panels and related equipment. While setting up your account, ask them who they would recommend to work for you doing part-time installations and service calls. A "contractors" alarm package cost around $100 and includes the alarm panel (computer hardware), 2 door sensors (front and back door) and 2 motion detectors. You can usually get a technician to install this for $100 - $200 so your entire cost to install a new alarm system is under $350. The more accounts you get, the more residual income you obtain each month. *I would caution you regarding your PI license. In some states, you may have to convert your PI license to include security related services.

CCTV systems - Closed Circuit TV systems (CCTV) are cameras that relay the signals to a digital video recorder (DVR). As you know, both businesses and homes use these types of camera systems. A 4-camera system can run from $2500 - $5000 depending on the quality of cameras and the amount of memory in the DVR. Additional concerns include 2-story houses that do not have access to an attic area between floors. Technicians that install burglar alarms are often trained to install CCTV systems.

Drug Screening - You may have employers that want to purchase drug screening panels to test employees and potential employees. They can send employees to a local medical clinic, have a nurse come to their location or purchase the drug screening panels and administer them onsite. The panels can test for a minimum of 4 drugs to panels that test for more than 20 different drugs. You can purchase the panels for as low as $4.95 wholesale and resell them for double or triple the price. Again this can be a simple pass-through where you don't actually maintain any inventory.

Pre-employment background screening - As mentioned earlier in the book, this can be a landmine if you are not careful. You can achieve some truly remarkable income through offering these services if set-up and handled correctly. Again this is a volume based service. You may make as little as .50 per search or as much as $5.00 but if you have a large volume this will easily make you a good living.

Security Consulting – This is an area that includes several sub-categories within this service area. You can provide vulnerability assessments to determine the lack of security within a business and make recommendations to remedy these issues. You can also conduct pre-construction and construction related consulting. In doing this, you work with the client to determine the level of security they need for their business. You incorporate the recommendations for cameras, card access readers, fencing, guard shacks, bollards, emergency lighting and similar equipment into the architectural drawings. The contract then uses this information to actual build the new building(s).

Locating Missing Heirs and Judgment Recovery – You can monitor the probate records at the courthouse and determine those cases where there are no known heirs. Through investigative research you may be able to determine living heirs and contract them to obtain a portion of the proceeds in return for helping the family locate and obtain the assets.

Electronic Countermeasures – This is often referred to as "bug sweeps" and is an investigative process for identifying listening devices, cameras and other intrusion devices in homes, businesses and cars. Unfortunately most PI's buy some cheap equipment and utilize this in an attempt to perform professional bug sweeps. Most of this equipment will only pick-up a small spectrum of wave lengths and miss more than they could ever find. If trained properly and through the use of the appropriate equipment, you can easily pick up jobs charging $1500 - $3500. I have done large jobs and made well over $100,000 on a single sweep.

Undercover Operatives – Often businesses suspect they have an internal theft or drug problem. To confirm their suspicions they will employee undercover operatives to act like an employee but they pay attention to the activity around them. These are normally longer in duration (6 weeks to 1 year) because it takes time to infiltrate clichés and gain the trust of fellow employees.

Mystery Shoppers – As part of quality control, many companies pay mystery shoppers to enter their establishment to determine the warmth of their employees, how they were treated, the speed and accuracy of the purchasing process and other such factors.

Each of these has the potential to supplement your primary investigation income as well as provide residual income. In doing so, you can become less sensitive to economic factors as you develop a better diversified income.

THE REAL SECRET TO SUCCESS
Chapter Fourteen

If you operate a successful business and make it look easy, everyone thinks they can do the same – or better. I have been blessed to have been recognized for much of my effort:

- #1 PI in the U.S. – PI Magazine
- #1 PI in the U.S. – NAIS
- PI of the Year – NAIS
- One of the Top PI's of the 20th Century – NAIS
- "One of the Most Successful PI's in the State of Texas" by Thomas Publications
- Editor/Publisher's Award by the National Assoc. of Legal Investigators
- "The Art of Surveillance" was chosen as the "Best Book of the Year for Surveillance Investigations" by the NAIS
- Past President (2010-2012) for TALI - the Texas Association of Licensed Investigators
- Board of Directors (2007-2010) for TALI
- Achieved the Texas Certified Investigator designation (less than 50 in TX.) – TALI
- Recipient of the 2013 Hudgins-Sallee award, the highest recognition presented by TALI
- Board of Directors for the Freedom of Information Foundation of Texas
- Public Relations committee for the Council of International Investigators
- Membership Chair for the San Antonio Chapter of ASIS
- Founding Board Member and Board Advisor for the non-profit organization "Can You Identify Me.
- Founder and President of the PI Institute of Education
- Founder and President of the Association of Christian Investigators
- Founder and President of the Coalition of Association Leaders (COAL)

As you can see, the private investigation profession has been good to me. Although *I* did not say I am the #1 PI, I certainly use this in my marketing. Also an important milestone is the fact that my business will have been in operation for 25 years as of April 2014. Business can be difficult, especially if you are not a Christian. I realize that God gave me talent, skills and favor. Even so, it is hard to follow a parked car. It has taken initiative and desire - and I have been blessed in my efforts. God is a gentleman. He will not invade your life. You have to ask him into your life. Likewise he cannot answer a prayer that has not been prayed. Even if you believe in Jesus Christ, that does not guarantee success in business. You still have to apply business principles and you still have to work hard.

I was destined to be a private investigator. I am fortunate in that I have never wanted to do anything else as far back as I can remember. This is what I am passionate about and it is much easier to put in the extra effort and the extra hours when it is your passion. My name, "Kelly" means defender or warrior and my last name "Riddle" means to discover hidden clues or solving a problem. "For I know the plans I have for you, declares the Lord, plans to prosper you and not to harm you, plans to give you hope and a future."[44] "Before I formed you in the womb I knew you, before you were born I set you apart."[45] It is clear that I am fulfilling the purpose in my life. Even so, God cannot bless those who will not work and who will not seek him. "A little sleep, a little slumber, a little folding of the hands to rest and poverty will come on you like a bandit."[46] Contrary to the reoccurring opinions, no one owes us anything and the government is certainly not our source. Hard work will be rewarded but like all things, this is a choice.

While I certainly appreciate the awards, I learned years ago to put things in perspective. "Whatever you do, work at it with all your heart, as working for the Lord, not for men, since you know that you will receive an inheritance from the Lord as a reward. It is the Lord Christ you are serving."[47] My pastor taught me long ago that if you want a bicycle; pray for a red bicycle with blue handlebars and yellow spokes so that there is absolutely no mistake that God answered your prayer.

I learned very quickly that my triumphs were because of God and in spite of me. "For the Lord gives wisdom, and from his mouth come knowledge and understanding. He holds victory in store for the upright, he is a shield to those whose walk is blameless, for he guards the course of the just and protects the way of his faithful ones."[48] The interesting thing about believing in God and the

---

[44] Jeremiah 29:11
[45] Jeremiah 1:5
[46] Proverbs 6:10
[47] Colossians 3:23-24
[48] Proverbs 2:6-8

blessings that come because of this belief is that it is literally so simple that it is hard. There are certain "principles" that must be met for all of the favor and blessings to enter your life:

1) Believe in Jesus Christ as Lord and Savior – "That if you confess with your mouth, "Jesus is Lord," and believe in your heart that God raised him from the dead, *you will be saved.* For it is with your heart that you believe and are justified, and it is with your mouth that you confess and are saved."[49] It doesn't say to walk 10 old ladies across the street or be the best person that ever lived. *Just believe* in Jesus Christ and all he did (John 3:16).

2) The next principle is to have *faith.* "I tell you the truth, if you have faith as small as a mustard seed, you can say to this mountain, "Move from here to there" and it will move. Nothing will be impossible for you." (Matthew 17:20). Further, "If you believe, you will receive whatever you ask for in prayer." (Matthew 21:22). This doesn't mean that God is a cosmic bellhop. You can't snap your fingers and have him respond to your every whim. It does mean that God will provide for you if your motives are right and pure.

3) The third is to give God the first fruits (tithe). God does not need your money but everything that God created gives. "Bring the whole tithe into the storehouse, that there may be food in my house. "Test me in this", says the Lord Almighty, "and see if I will not throw open the floodgates of heaven and pour out so much blessing that you will not have room enough for it. I will prevent pests from devouring your crops, and the vines in your fields will not cast their fruit," says the Lord Almight."[50] This is the only place in the Bible where God says "*test me.*" It is not your money he wants but your discipline, respect and love.

This is a very basic explanation of how God works in a believer's life. I can tell you without a shadow of a doubt that God wants to give you favor and blessings. The problem is most people do not know how to pray and once done, do not have sufficient faith to see it through. "The effectual fervent prayer of a righteous man availeth much."[51] In Hebrews Chapter 11, faith is mentioned 28

---

[49] Romans 10:9-10
[50] Malachi 3:10-11
[51] James 5:16

times just in this chapter. It is a reoccurring theme throughout the bible. "Now faith is being sure of what we hope for and certain of what we do not see" (Hebrews 11:1). Everyone has faith in something. If it is not in God, then you will be disappointed at some point and whatever your faith is in will fail. God is the same yesterday, today and forever. Again, this seems so easy that it can be hard. "Whatever is has already been, and what will be has been before; and God will call the past to account."[52] So if others have been successful, if others have been victorious than why not me or you? The difference is the ability to combine faith with action. The difference is being able to pray strong prayers of certainty and not be wishy-washy in your thinking or belief structure.

This would be a good point to say that I am not a preacher. I acknowledged and accepted Jesus Christ as my Savior at the age of 12. Since that time I have continued to read the bible again and again. Through the reading and the hearing of God's word it became ingrained in my personality and makeup. You seldom will hear my "preach" as I chose to lead by example. I did create the Association of Christian Investigators (www.a-c-i.org) in an attempt to give like-minded PI's the ability to connect with others with similar beliefs and to increase the integrity within our profession.

The things I have accomplished are not by accident. I have prayed for success, favor and opportunities. I have asked God for wisdom and to strengthen me to carry out the tasks needed to succeed. In doing so, I have a tremendous desire to excel in this profession. A person can only go so far under the own steam. The fact that 83% of PI agencies are 1 or 2 person operations and that over 60% are no longer in business within 5 years speaks volumes regarding the accomplishments listed at the start of this chapter. God expects us to give him the glory and to not take it and say "Look what I have done." All things good give God the creator glory. I can only ask you to let the facts speak. I am thankful that God has ordered my footsteps.

My concluding statements are based on my experience. If you are going to do something, do it with all your heart and strength. Business is difficult and you will not be able to do it alone. Without God it is simply a waste of time but "with God all things are possible."[53]

---

[52] Ecclesiastes 3:15
[53] Philippians 4:13

ABOUT THE AUTHOR
Chapter Fifteen

Professional Experience Narrative: Mr. Riddle has more than 35 years of investigative experience and earned a Bachelor of Science degree in Criminal Justice from the University of North Alabama. He was chosen as the **"PI of the Year"** by the National Association of Investigative Specialists and the PI Magazine named Mr. Riddle as the **"#1 PI in the United States"**. He has been designated an expert in surveillance, insurance investigations, nursing home abuse and computer investigations. He was chosen as **"One of the Top 25 PI's of the 20th Century."** Kelly obtained his **Texas Certified Investigator** designation (less than 50 in TX.) Mr. Riddle is also the past **President (2010-2012) for TALI** - the Texas Association of Licensed Investigators (TALI); **Board of Directors (2007-2010) for TALI** as well as being on the Board of Directors for the **Freedom of Information Foundation of Texas**. Kelly is on the Public Relations committee for the **Council of International Investigators** and the Membership Chair for the San Antonio Chapter of ASIS. He is a Founding Board Member and Board Advisor for the non-profit organization "Can You Identify Me." Kelly was the recipient of the **2013 Hudgins-Sallee award**, the highest recognition presented by the Texas Association of Licensed Investigators.

Mr. Riddle is the author of 10 books and has published more than 40 articles. He has been the guest speaker at more than 400 events and has been on national TV, radio and newspapers.

Prior law enforcement experience includes being a member of the SWAT team, a Training Officer, Emergency Medical Technician, Evidence Technician, Arson Investigator, Juvenile Specialist and Traffic Investigator.

Mr. Riddle is the Founder and President of the **PI Institute of Education**, as well as the **Association of Christian Investigators** with more than 1000 members in the U.S. and 19 countries. Kelly is the Founder of the **Coalition of Association Leaders** comprised of past and present board members from state, national and international associations.

Mr. Riddle is a member of NAIS,TALI,ASIS,NALI,FAPI,LAPI, USAPI,ACI, NAAA,PICA,WIN, NLLI, CTIB, CLEAR,IOPIA,TIDA,CII,ASSIST

For more information, please review our websites at www.kelmarpi.com, www.a-c-i.com and www.PIinstitute.com.   You may reach Mr. Riddle via the Internet at the e-mail address of Kelly@KelmarGlobal.com.

 Kelly E. Riddle

Other Products by Kelly E. Riddle

- Book: "Private Investigating Made Easy"

- Book: "Insurance Investigations from A to Z"

- Book: "The Art of Surveillance"

- Book: "Security Consulting for the 21st Century Consultant"

- Book: "Investigating Nursing Home Abuse"

- Book: "Exposed – True Cases of America's #1 PI"

- Book: "The Internet Black Book"

For more information, contact Kelly E. Riddle at (210) 342-0509 or e-mail at Kelly@KelmarGlobal.com

Made in the USA
Monee, IL
26 February 2021